In Defence of Serendipity

Praise for *In Defence of Serendipity*

"I was deeply moved by this melancholy work, which sums up a generation of hectic labor by so many of my innovative friends and colleagues. Yes, the Digital Revolution has eaten its young, as indeed most revolutions do. It went from movement, to business, to racket, and if you read Seb Olma, you'll have an inkling of how and why that happened, and what must come next."

Bruce Sterling, sci-fi writer and futurist

"In this practice-driven and original essay, Sebastian Olma successfully catapults dialectics into the heart of the brutal 'creative industry' rhetoric. Good luck picking up the bits and pieces after the blast!"

Geert Lovink, net critic

"Sebastian Olma's timely meditation on the uses and abuses of serendipity sets out to free chance invention and accidental discovery from its corporate and state captivity in the 'creative industries'. His defence of serendipity as a sagacity of resistance dedicated to an open future is made with a wit and lightness of spirit conspicuously absent in the lugubrious managerialist appropriations of the term. His erudite polemic convinces the reader that – as Pasteur might now say – chance favours the mind prepared to change."

Howard Caygill, philosopher

SEBASTIAN OLMA

In Defence of Serendipity

For A Radical Politics
of Innovation

Published by Repeater Books

An imprint of Watkins Media Ltd
19-21 Cecil Court
London
WC2N 4EZ
UK

www.repeaterbooks.com
A Repeater Books paperback original 2016
1

Distributed in the United States by Random House, Inc., New York.

ISBN: 978-1-910924-34-1
Ebook ISBN: 978-1-910924-35-8

Cover design: Johnny Bull
Typography and typesetting: Jan Middendorp
Typefaces: Chaparral Pro, Absara Sans
Printed and bound in Finland

Contents

The Great Digital Swindle

by Mark Fisher

Who dares dissent from the gospel according to Silicon Valley? There is – we are insistently told – no alternative to the invasion of capitalist cyberspace into all areas of consciousness and culture. Anyone who expresses even the mildest scepticism about social media and smartphones is roundly denounced as nostalgic. The old, desperate not to seem out of touch, rarely dare question the young's compulsive attachment to their smartphones. Anti-capitalists join with tycoons to celebrate the potentials of network society. In article after article, conference after conference, the "new" is routinely equated with "the digital", to such an extent that is now difficult to remember a time when "technology" wasn't a shorthand for communicative software. When mobile phones entered the marketplace, they were the object of mockery: who could be so self-important as to believe that they needed to be contactable everywhere and anywhere? Now, everyone is required to act like some cross between a hustler always on the make and an addict jonesing for contact.

But how has this model of progress, in which history culminates in the glorious invention of iPhones and apps, become so uncontested? And, if we attend closely, isn't there a desperate quality to all this cheerleading? Addicts always rationalise their compulsions, but the desperation here belongs to capital itself, which has thrown everything at the great digital swindle. Capital might still swagger like some data cowboy, but iPhones plus Victorian values can only be a steampunk throwback. The return to centuries' old forms of exploitation is obfuscated by the distracting urgencies of digital communication.

What if Silicon Valley was not – as we are relentlessly hectored to believe – a stupendous success story, but a massive monument to failure? *In Defence of Serendipity* encourages us to pose this counter-intuitive question. Sebastian Olma demonstrates that neoliberal capitalism has systematically destroyed the conditions which allowed Silicon Valley to emerge, at the very same time as it pimps 70s California as the definitive model for all cultural as well as business innovation. In Olma's narrative, Steve Jobs and the other Californian oligarchs come to seem like the hapless figures from a fairy tale. They wished to totally transform the world, but instead they received unimaginable wealth. Their devices only led to more of the same: the "changeless change" of a capitalism that endlessly crows about innovation in a manic attempt to cover over the glacial monotony of its homogeneity and repetitiveness. The Silicon Valley princes provided capital with new tools of capture and captivation. More than that, they gave capital a new hymn sheet, a way to sell drudgery as creativity and hyper-exploitation as sharing, so that we are all expected to be "passionate" about our cyber-serfery.

It is by now screamingly clear that innovation does not spontaneously effloresce when capital dominates society and culture. Generalised insecurity leads to sterility and repetition, not surprise and innovation. The conditions in which the new can appear have to be produced and nurtured. This, Sebastian Olma demonstrates, is the real import of the concept of serendipity when it is properly understood. The irony of Silicon Valley is that its very hegemonic dominion has contributed to the disappearance of such conditions in the capitalist world. Silicon Valley emerged from the serendipitous synthesis of the counterculture and state-sponsored cybernetics, but neoliberal capital has destroyed the possibility of a counterculture even as it has annexed and subdued the state. *In Defence of Serendipity* shows that that the real future is building itself beyond the instrumentalising urgencies of business, in the spaces between a new bohemia and a revived public sphere.

Serendipity, Innovation and the Question of the Future

1. In Defence of Serendipity

Serendipity is a unique term in the English language describing the process by which one finds something useful, valuable or just generally 'good' without actually looking for it. Throughout the history of invention and discovery serendipity has functioned as a sort of Freudian unconscious, leading – or perhaps better, tricking – the curious human mind onto unexpected novelty. And yet, it is only recently that we are becoming truly aware of the crucial role serendipity plays in our attempts to creatively grasp toward the future. Over the last few years, it has become an important, if not overused, reference for the creative industries, as well as for our innovation-obsessed economy in general. This is remarkable as 'serendipity' was originally conceived in the middle of the 18th century within literary circles, where it led its marginal existence until very recently. Horace Walpole, art historian and eccentric son of the first British Prime Minister, coined the term in 1754. He had come across the "silly fairy tale" *Peregrinaggio di tre giovani figliuoli del re di Serendippo*, which was the Italian translation of the ancient Persian parable of the three princes of Serendip, the Persian name for Sri Lanka.[1] The king had sent his sons on a

---

1 Lewis 1937-83: 407. Michele Tramezzino published the Italian translation in Venice in 1557. English translations exist but seem to be out of print. A renarration of the tale by Richard Boyle can be found here: http://livingheritage.org/serendipity.htm.

punitive expedition for having refused succeeding him after their education. As Walpole writes, during their travels the smart royal kids "were always making discoveries, by accidents and sagacity, of things they were not in quest of...".[2] This became Walpole's definition of his newly coined term *serendipity* and as such, it spread through the world of literates and bibliophiles. Scientists, of course, were always able to relate to the term, as it describes pretty much the principle of scientific discoveries and inventions. Louis Pasteur's often-cited adage about chance favouring only prepared minds is only the most famous statement as to serendipity's significance for the world of science.

Today, serendipity has left the libraries and academic circles in order to start a new life in a society that doesn't seem to tire of its endless chatter on innovation. As a term that almost lyrically articulates the strange occurrence of an unexpected finding, serendipity is quickly becoming an important reference for those whose profession it is to make our economies more innovative, our industries and cities more creative, and our future, well, better. Within the creative industries, with their co-working spaces, creative hubs and start-up centres, the notion has become a guiding reference for the new generation of freelancers and entrepreneurs for whom the principle of valuable unexpected encounters (of new ideas for products and services, funding opportunities, contracts, business partners, etc.) is something like the foundation of economic survival.[3] For popular nonfiction authors and

2 Ibid.: 408.

3 E.g., Johns & Gratton 2013. Academics working in the areas of organisation and management studies, as well as in the social sciences, are slowly picking up on this phenomenon. The reason why I abstained from providing more than the one HBR reference here is that the proper academic work on this issue tends to be of excruciating triviality. For those interested in an up-to-date (yet free of any critical reflection) picture of this world, I'd suggest to go to the online magazine deskmag.com.

academics working within the field of the creative industries, serendipity is often instrumental for understanding the dynamics of 'creativity'. Think, for instance, of the way in which scholars such as Richard Florida or Charles Landry conceptualise their vision of the creative city. Yet, in this wonderful world of TED, PechaKucha and awesome one-liners, it should not be surprising that serendipity is quickly becoming a fad. This is unfortunate as I believe that the notion offers more than meets the Google-glassed eye. I would therefore like to suggest that we begin our investigation by looking into serendipity more thoroughly than is usually done so.

2. Understanding Serendipity: Troubled Etymology

Let's start with a bit of etymology, then. We know about the moment of Walpole's coining of serendipity from a letter in which he shares his linguistic invention with his friend Horace Mann, who had just sent him a portrait of the Grand Duchess Bianca Capello. Walpole uses this occasion to report to Mann on a "critical discovery" he just made about the Capello arms in an old book of Venetian arms. This discovery, he writes, was one of the kinds of "accidental sagacity" for which he is happy to have created his neologism.

Although today Walpole is mainly remembered as a trendsetter for the Victorian revival of the Gothic – by virtue of Strawberry Hill, his neo-Gothic home he built in Twickenham, South West London, as well his Gothic novel *The Castel of Otranto* – he was also a reluctant politician and active publisher. His numerous letters were posthumously published and are seen today as a valuable source of historical documentation. Besides, they also testify to Walpole's talent and wittiness as a communicator. The 18th century, of course, was a time in which the nobility distinguished itself through the display of conversational skill. The salons of London and Paris provided the stages for 'great conversation', as did the art of written correspondence. Walpole was very much part of this world, a great conversationalist and inventor of many a neologism. In this sense, his invention of the term serendipity was certainly no accident.

Yet, there is something rather confusing in his letter to Horace Mann, and this confusion results from the very story of the three princes from which Walpole derives his new word. The puzzling fact is that the story of *Peregrinaggio di tre giovani figliuoli del re di Serendippo* itself does not at all convey the sense of 'finding the unexpected' through a combination of accident and sagacity. In fact, the tale resembles much more what today we would call a detective story than, say, an unintended treasure hunt. The princes impress the locals they meet on their travels with their wittiness, great powers of observation and intuition, skills that lead them to all sorts of smart inferences and deductions. They also save Emperor Beramo from being poisoned by one of his counsellors (and later from a broken heart) and solve a great metaphysical riddle for a "virgin queen". They do not, however, make any unexpected discoveries or unsought findings. Indeed, nowhere in this fairy tale do we find anything close to the notion of serendipity that Walpole seems to intend when he defines it in terms of "*accidental sagacity* (for you must observe that *no* discovery of a thing you *are* looking for comes under this description)".[4]

This is equally true for the part of the *Peregrinaggio* that most impressed our language artist, i.e., the story of the camel. Pek van Andel provides a great summary of this fragment, which I quote here for the sake of convenience, in its entirety:

One day they walked along the track of a camel. The eldest brother saw that the grass on the left side of the track was grazen bare, while the sappy grass on the right was undisturbed. He concluded

4   Lewis 1937-83: 408.

that the camel's right eye was blind. The middle brother observed in the left verge many plugs of chewn grass. That gave him the idea the camel might miss a tooth. The youngest brother inferred from the relative faint imprint that the left back leg of the camel was crippled. Further on, the eldest brother noticed on one side of the track over a distance of a mile an endless stream of ants consuming something and on the other side a vast mass of bees, flies and wasps nibbling a transparent sticky stuff. He gathered that the camel was loaded on one side with butter and with honey on the other. The second brother discovered traces indicating that the animal had kneeled. He also found there marks of small human feet and a wet spot. He touched it with his fingers and even before smelling them he felt a carnal temptation. He concluded that a woman sat on the camel. Handprints on both sides of the place where she had watered were noticed by the third brother. The woman had supported herself because of the size of her body and might be pregnant, he thought. Later the three brothers met a camel driver, who missed one of his animals. Because they had seen so many tracks they joked that they had seen the camel and to make it credible they mentioned the seven marks, which all appeared right. Accused of theft the brothers were put in jail. But the unharmed camel was found and they were released. After many other travels and adventures they succeeded their father in Serendip.[5]

Again, we encounter inference and observation but nothing that would ground the logical derivation of the term in the story of the three princes. What the princes do is demonstrate great wit; they are extremely smart and conduct themselves with great courtesy and modesty, which is something that doubtlessly appealed to the English nobleman. It was probably Walpole's sympathy for

5   Van Andel 1994: 632.

what he took to be three men of his kind, combined with a certain Oriental fashion of the time – derived, not least, from European commercial and political involvement in Asia – that made the story stand out to him. Perhaps he even thought of his act of linguistic innovation as a practical continuation of the three princes' ancient royal wit.

In *The Travels and Adventures of Serendipity*, sociologists Robert K. Merton and Elinor Barber have beautifully reconstructed the historical trajectory of the term. They are puzzled too by the etymological confusion around Walpole's inception of serendipity, which they discuss in much greater detail than would be appropriate in these preliminary remarks. The authors find their way out of this conundrum with reference to the importance of Walpole's experience as an eclectic collector of art and, most importantly, books. This particular occupation, they argue, must have coloured his reading of the parable of the three princes. And this is also the very likely reason why serendipity was taken up and spread at first in particular through the circles of collectors, antiquarians and bibliophiles. For the collectors, Merton and Barber muse, serendipity "described that unknown quantity that intervened between [their] assiduous efforts and certain success". As they continue:

All collectors are familiar with different aspects of this experience, the recurrent discrepancy between efforts and results. The experience may take the form of a windfall, of a valuable item that 'just drops into one's lap', as it were; or, conversely, it may take the form of an endless, devoted, and ever-unsuccessful pursuit of a valued item; or, finally, and most commonly, the discrepancy between efforts and results may be less extreme than the totally unexpected windfall or the ever-elusive Grail, yet 'just a little bit of luck', good or bad, will make a great deal of difference to the satisfactory outcome of a collector's enterprise. In a collector's life

the conditions of success are to an unusual extent unknowable, and
the notion of serendipity (whatever its particular interpretation
may be [...]) serves to make some sense out of this uncertainty.[6]

Hence, what Walpole's explanation of serendipity obscures, his
occupational experience as a collector brings back to light. Serendipity for Walpole is inextricably connected to his life as a collector. It is that which intervenes in between the effort of searching
for something valuable and the eventual result of this search. It
articulates the accidental sagacious efforts needed in order to be
thrown off the beaten path and led into the unchartered territory
where the 'new' – understood here in terms of something relevant
to the collector that previously had been overlooked – is hiding.
Inversely, such an accident requires the informed intuition of the
collector that enables him or her to lift the accidentally found 'old
data' into its meaningful new context. As Pasteur is going to say
exactly one century after Walpole's invention of serendipity, the
relevant accident presents itself only to those who make such a
sagacious effort: "Chance only favours prepared minds".

Yet before the notion of serendipity as such enters the minds
of scientists, almost two centuries are going to pass. Merton and
Barber's description of the puzzling and confused emergence of
the term illustrates the birth defect of serendipity that creates
the etymological fuzziness leading to the diversity of interpretations that the notion affords until this day. By creating this "very
expressive word"[7] on a whim, Walpole gave us an enormously rich
term that took on a life of its own while traveling through the centuries and spreading through different social groups and cultures.
Today, it is returning with a significance that its inventor could
not have had even the slightest premonition of.

6   Ibid.: 124-125.
7   Lewis 1937-83: 407.

Walpole's correspondence was published posthumously in 1833. The early Victorian literates, however, proved way too serious to appreciate his eclectic style, not to mention his obscure linguistic creation 'serendipity'. Its travels and adventures only take off with the 'bibliomaniacs' of the later Victorian period, when the literary *dilettantes* and amateur scholars begin to discover the term. Leading their readers through the serendipitous labyrinths of collectors, booksellers, writers, literary scholars, lexicographers and medical humanists, Merton and Barber eventually arrive at the world of scientific and academic research.

3. Serendipity Pattern: Accident & Sagacity

Once Merton and Barber turn their attention toward science, it becomes clear that much more is at stake in their story than a whimsical etymology of a strange linguistic phenomenon. James Shulman, in his introduction to *The Travels and Adventures of Serendipity*, provides an excellent lead regarding the motivation for the authors' scholarly application to this particular piece of etymological obscurity. "In that it emblematizes the Eureka moment in its distilled form", Shulman writes, "serendipity can be read as a synecdoche for all the ambiguities of the process of discovery more broadly considered." [8]

Indeed, what Merton and Barber are after is a lateral entry into the theory of scientific knowledge creation. They believe that serendipity can serve as a conceptual tool, addressing the inherent ambiguities of scientific creativity without either diminishing the integrity of the scientist or attacking the necessity of planned and structured research. Instead, they are looking for the mechanics behind the process of scientific discovery. Merton and Barber find

8 Merton & Barber 2004: XVI.

these mechanics in what they call the "serendipity pattern".[9] The serendipity pattern describes the logic of what happens when the observation of *unanticipated, anomalous and strategic* data (or, as they have it, a singular "datum") leads to a discovery, a new theory, or the extension of an existing one. Serendipity is understood here as a sort of triple jump, starting with the occurrence of an unanticipated piece of data. First jump: a research effort directed toward the test of a particular hypothesis yields an unexpected observation bearing upon theories that were not initially questioned by the research. Second jump: apparently inconsistent with prevailing knowledge, the unexpected observation raises the curiosity of the scientist who tries to make sense of it. Third jump: the scientist inquires into the possible implications – destructive or expansive – the unexpected data has on an existing body of knowledge.

Merton and Barber's serendipity pattern provides us with a snapshot of the moment when the complex ingredients necessary for discovery converge on this one point in space and time through which the new enters into the world. However, this snapshot was taken as early as the 1940s, predating the post-war debates on the nature of scientific truth claims. Their 'discovery' of the serendipity pattern therefore displays an innocence that is untouched by the academic crossfire that social constructivism, post-structuralism, actor-network theory, and a number of other camps have exchanged since. It is, luckily, not our task here to throw serendipity into these academic trenches. It seems to me that much more can be gained by using the momentum of the serendipitous triple jump to leap out of the context of scientific research altogether and into the realm of contemporary economy and culture. Such a move seems justified to me as long as we do not pretend that the serendipity pattern presents a full-blown

9   Ibid.: 195-198.

and exhaustive theory of discovery – scientific or otherwise. It is quite clear that this was not at all Merton and Barber's intention and neither is it mine. Rather, I would like to take it as a point of departure from which an investigation into the contemporary conditions for innovation can be launched. The significance of the notion of serendipity that can be extracted from Merton and Barber's pattern lies in its ability to articulate the structure of an important dimension of human creativity condensed into one crucial event.

What we get from Merton and Barber – which is something that was already present in Walpole's initial formulation of serendipity in terms of accidental sagacity – is a basic pattern of discovery made up of two crucial dimensions: accident and sagacity. The first dimension, *accident*, stands for the unanticipated occurrence of an anomalous set or piece of data. The second dimension, *sagacity*, denotes the ability of the researcher to recognise the anomaly as such, make sense of it and turn it into a creative alteration of the existing body of knowledge. Serendipity, one might say, is what happens when both accident and sagacity connect in space and time, with novelty as their outcome.

While even in a laboratory setting, there is a host of contingent factors that feed into the serendipity pattern, from the instruments producing the data to the diverse internal and external influences on the researcher – outside the laboratory things get a lot messier. To begin with, there is not necessarily an intentionally controlled relationship between observer and data. When serendipity happens in the real world, the 'unanticipated data' tend to emerge out of the conjuncture of ideas, objects, intuitions, knowledge fragments, etc., that in the usual course of things would not encounter each other. In fact, the history of discoveries, inventions and innovations since Archimedes' Eureka moment in the bath tub can be read as an endless chain of such unexpected encounters while taking a stroll, relaxing for a bit from work or just generally directing one's senses for a change in an unusual direction. This is the moment that one becomes part of what contemporary philosophers working in the tradition of Friedrich Nietzsche, Henri Bergson and Gilles Deleuze refer to as a virtual multiplicity: a set of relations is formed, accidentally harbouring the potential for novelty that is 'unanticipated' insofar as it carries an anomalous datum. Yet, just as in the laboratory, somewhere within the unexpected set of relationships there has to be a consciousness with the curiosity and the ability to recognize the potential value of this newly emerged multiplicity. This is, then, the second dimension of serendipity, *sagacity*, where the potential gets embodied, where the virtual multiplicity is actualised and enters into the 'real' or actual world. Without this second dimension, serendipity does not work, which is to say that the act of creation does not take place. Sagacity is where the depth of experience, expertise, craftsmanship, etc. enter into the game, initiating the creative process by which unexpected encounters acquire their novelty value. So serendipity needs both the multiplicity of the unexpected encounter (accident) and the creative act (sagacity) actualising the encounter for and into the world.

Serendipity thus articulates the event of discovery or invention understood as the precondition for innovation. It is in this sense that serendipity can be taken to describe an important nexus through which what the Greeks called *poïesis* takes place: the ontological process of something passing from nonbeing into being. In Plato's *Symposium*, Diotima of Mantinea explains to Socrates that the cause of something passing from not being into being is called *poïesis*. What Diotima wants to make clear is that every production as activity that brings something into the world is *poïesis*, even though the name has come to be reserved for the particular activity within the arts that is called poetry. In the *Nicomachean Ethics*, Aristotle opposes the notion of *poïesis* to that of *praxis*: "[T]he genus of action [*praxis*] is different from that of production [*poïesis*], for production [*poïesis*] has an end other than itself, but action [*praxis*] does not: good action is itself an end." [10] In other words, *poïesis* is the process that generates something new. In Aristotle's definition it is that which has its end and limit outside itself. *Poïesis* is thus always in material excess of itself, whereas praxis remains immanent to itself.

Serendipity takes the creative process of *poïesis*, i.e., the kind of creative process at whose end something new will have entered the world, and compresses it into the incident where it really happens. This gives us a sort of minimalist mechanism through which the creative human ability to create novelty can be approached. Serendipity by itself does not of course provide anything close to a theory of creativity, but it gives us a basic mechanics of the moment when genuine novelty is born, when *poïesis* throws something new into the world through that opening produced by the synchronicity of accident and sagacity.

But let's take another, even closer look at the two dimensions of serendipity, one that gets us even further away from the laboratory context. The first dimension, accident, stands for an unintended departure from the usual course of things. In the first instance, we might understand this swerve from the ordinary in the sense of what Lucretius in his beautiful poem *De Rerum Natura* calls the *clinamen*: a deviation from the laminar movement of atoms causing a vortex out of which something new might emerge. [11] In the 20th century, of course, Lucretius' Greco-Roman atomism has experienced its popular modernisation by the theory of complexity. [12] Applying complexity theory's

10 Aristotle 1941: VI 1140b.

11 On the somewhat serendipitous story of the discovery of *De Rerum Natura* – Lucretius' celebration of the Greek philosopher Epicurus, who, in many ways, anticipated the discoveries of modern science – see Greenblatt 2011.

12 The classic reading here is Prigogine & Stenger 1984.

insights to the dimension of social life, we could say that the deviation is caused by an extraordinary conjuncture of ideas, objects, intuitions, knowledge fragments, etc. As I said above, I would like to approach this dimension of serendipity in terms of what contemporary philosophers refer to as virtual multiplicity: these are relations forming a potential prior to any subjective or objective embodiment. Multiplicity is the philosophical expression of an ontological network consisting of relations – forces, affects, desires – that don't yet have what we might call social efficacy. They have a latent meaning that still requires a creative (sagacious) act in order to become actualised (as something new, an innovation, etc.). Nonetheless, the virtual dimension of accidents is real; it represents the essential precondition for the new to actually emerge.

Which brings us to serendipity's second dimension: sagacity. This is where the potential that emerged within the virtual multiplicity gets embodied, where it is actualised and effectively enters into the world. Here is where the magic happens, except that it isn't magical at all. In fact, the creative act is essentially one of *resistance*. This is to say that the accident acquires social efficacy through the sagacious realisation that something new is potentially occurring, followed by an act of resisting the alignment of this occurrence with the existing vectors of knowledge and power. In other words, he or she resists the temptation of going down the path of *least resistance* in favour of a sagacious effort. In science, the responsibility for the sagacious act rests on the shoulder of the scientist who observes an anomalous datum and follows its lead rather than trying to ignore it or force it under an existing theory. However, this doesn't mean that sagacity is a question of an autonomous individual mindset, as the scientist who recognises the relevance of the anomaly and turns it into a discovery or invention has been shaped by a communal ethics of scientific curiosity. Rather, sagacity is the expression of what Lucretius defined as the joy of advancing our understanding in the "nature of things," the joy, as Gilles Deleuze would say, of accomplishing a moment of *le survol*, i.e., of being in sync with the creative movement of becoming. Which is to say that we need to define sagacity as an act of joyous resistance that pushes the world forward.

4. The Problem: Future in Hiding

The problem we are facing today is that our infrastructures of innovation are programmed in such a way that they are neither susceptible to accidents of the disruptively generative kind nor particularly hospitable to the kind of sagacity that would recognise *disruptive* potential – understood strictly in the non-Californian sense of the term. True, we constantly talk about disruption and innovation, yet at the same time, we feel that our societies have become subject to an overwhelming stasis. Which is exactly why we are obsessed with innovation. Charles Leadbeater, one of Europe's chief innovation gurus, is asking the question: "Could we now live in an era where the economy is stagnating in part because there is so much innovation?" [13] And he is partly right; although there certainly is no shortage of new patents and technological inventions, something seems to prevent them from feeding into social processes of innovation proper. In other words, the problem is not, as Leadbeater seems to think, too much innovation, but rather the predominance of strangely parochial approaches to innovation that stage the spectacle of the upgrade (which, from a non-technological perspective, often entails a factual downgrade) as actual disruption. The stasis many of us perceive today is closely linked to this lack of ambition regarding innovation understood as a process of qualitative change.

One of the areas particularly vulnerable to the charge of

13 Leadbeater 2015.

innovation inertia is contemporary pop culture. British philosopher and cultural critic Mark Fisher is an important voice in
this debate, highlighting the repetitiveness of, above all, popular music culture. This is not, he argues, a question of the 'old'
recoiling from the 'new' in the sense of a previous young and now
ageing generation failing to come to terms with the new 'new'.
According to Fisher, our current pop culture gives ample evidence
that the ageist assumption that young equals culturally progressive is now out of date. There seems to be a lack of cultural new-
ness that he illustrates beautifully by placing himself in an imaginary time machine:

> Imagine any record released in the past couple of years being
> beamed back in time to, say, 1995 and played on the radio. It's hard
> to think that it will produce any jolt in the listeners. On the
> contrary, what would be likely to shock our 1995 audience would
> be the very recognisability of the sounds: would music really have
> changed so little in the next 17 years? Contrast this with the rapid
> turnover of styles between the 1960s and the 90s: play a jungle
> record from 1993 to someone in 1989 and it would have sounded
> like something so new that it would have challenged them to
> rethink what music was, or could be. While 20th-century experi-
> mental culture was seized by a *recombinatorial delirium*, which
> made it feel as if newness was infinitely available, the 21st century
> is oppressed by a crushing sense of finitude and exhaustion. It
> doesn't feel like the future.[14]

While some readers may find that the spirit of *Kulturpessimismus*
has a certain presence in Fisher's writing, I don't think it can be
reduced to that. What he seems to be saying, and rightly so, is that
there is no good reason to assume for innovation to be distributed

14 Fisher 2014: 7-8, emphasis added.

evenly across history. We simply live, as Fisher argues against received wisdom, in particularly un-innovative times. Serendipity might increasingly be the talk of the town, but it doesn't manifest in anything like the "recombinatorial delirium" Fisher refers to – neither in popular music nor, I am afraid to say, anywhere else.

Perhaps surprisingly, this kind of reasoning also registers with those whose very *business* is the future. Veteran futurist and trend watcher Matthias Horx, for instance, identifies our present cultural condition as *Gegenwartseitelkeit*, i.e., presentist narcissism.[15] The constant chatter about innovation, disruption and creativity remains credible only to those who believe that our time has to be unprecedentedly innovative by virtue of being the latest edition of the present. Yet, *kairos*, according to Greek philosophy the tip of the arrow of time, seems to have become blunt. Clayton Christensen, Harvard Business School professor and high priest of market disruption, believes that capitalism is losing its creative momentum thanks to its entrenchment in the matrices of finance. The regressive logic of finance prevents economic actors from investing in potentially disruptive products and services. What is most interesting about Christensen's argument in *The Capitalist's Dilemma* is that it links the current innovative impotence to business' increasing inability to serve society. Thanks to its thorough financialisation, the economic game has become so radically self-referential that even Niklas Luhmann would be shocked. The result of this economic hermeticism is not just soaring social inequality, as bemoaned by Thomas Piketty. It also cuts off economic rationality from the diversity of non-economic inputs that are necessary to move the economy forward. It's almost like in the olden days, towards the end of the Eastern Bloc: while the global party press (TED, Wired, O'Reilly, etc.) runs hot churning out the

---

15 Quoted in Friebe 2014: 87. Friebe's book itself is an entertaining take down of the current obsession with change as well!

credo of the innovation economy, the hiatus between the image of the world according to the innovation gospel and real existing stasis is becoming so great that even the true believers are starting to doubt.

We encounter this predicament also within the realm of technology itself. In *The Utopia of Rules*, the American Anthropologist David Graeber files a complaint against the absence of truly awesome innovations, such as flying cars and robot factories. Technology pundits and futurists promised their arrival decades ago but so far, they don't seem to have materialised. Certainly, tech-savvy readers might point to existing prototypes and the developments in the field of Smart Technology or Industry 4.0. Yet, one is bound to give at least some credit to Graeber's scepticism in a time where the icon of innovative consumer tech is a pimped digital wristwatch and the pinnacle of the experience economy consists of a car robbing the customer of the experience of driving. And while the personal computer has given us things like the paperless office, Graeber argues, its effect on management processes broadly speaking has much less been digital disruption for the sake of efficiency than the increase of the very bureaucratic obesity neoliberalism promised to eradicate. Today's bureaucracies – both public and private – run on a managerial operating system of Digital Taylorism that has introduced an extra layer of consultants and bureaucrats whose procrustean task is to trim professional activities to the standards of the relevant software. One of the perfidies of this system is that it combines urgent requests for creative, innovative and, indeed, serendipitous behaviour with a managerial infrastructure making exactly this impossible. The frustration generated by the daily experience of being trapped between constant demands for creative self-actualisation and a professional infrastructure effectively preventing anything close to it obviously has an effect on our individual and collective psyches. Where stasis is promoted in the name of innovation, it becomes increasingly difficult to even imagine a possible beyond.

This problem is increasingly recognised in design-related fields as well. Harald Welzer, Germany's authority on transformation design and author of *Selber Denken* (*Think for Yourself*), speaks of the dominance of an unfortunate tunnel vision when it comes to imagining the future. His analysis operates with a fairly wide and ethically cut lens, locating the innovation problem with capitalism's systematic insistence on growth that is not just ecologically dangerous but also boringly self-referential. It's not getting us anywhere new, he argues, but instead shoving more and more down our throats and up our brains, making us humongous in every sense – like the Mini Cooper turning into a shopping tank. The future disappears under the consumerist flab of the present.

An even more pessimistic take on our present problems with the future comes from the Italian philosopher Franco (Bifo) Berardi. According to the title of his book on the issue, we are already living *After the Future*. He diagnoses a veritable futurelessness of the present as the result of a digitally induced regression of our anthropological capacity for what he calls "conjunction", or, as we might say, sociability. Georg Simmel, one of the fathers of the discipline of sociology, defined the impulse to sociability in human beings as the drive to create "associations... [through which] the solitariness of the individual is resolved into togetherness, a union with others".[16] This capacity to move from solitariness to solidarity, Berardi claims, is what we are in the process of losing. Swimming constantly in what Nicholas Carr branded "the shallows" of digital information titbits, human beings in the 21st century are departing from the political animal Aristotle once spoke of. And this is causing our loss of future because "conjunction is becoming-other",[17] as Berardi says, meaning that one

16 Simmel 1999: 106.
17 Berardi 2010: 37.

needs to be able to meaningfully connect to one another in order to change one's standpoint, i.e., move forward into one's own future. The individual is literally wrapped in a cloud of pseudo-information (think quantified self), inhibiting the emergence of the abstract solidarity that is fundamental to society as a future-directed project. German-Korean philosopher Byung-Chul Han has made a similar argument in his book on *Psychopolitik*, referring to digital media in terms of a narcissistic surface or mirror turning the individual into a perpetual loop of proto-pathological self-reference.

While there can be no doubt as to the detrimental effects of the massive use and, indeed, abuse of digital media on our individual and collective psyches, putting the blame on technology *per se* is less than convincing. It is certainly true that our relationship to the digital in the context of innovation and creativity merits close analysis, and I hope to contribute modestly to such an analysis throughout the chapters of this book. However, in its essence, digital technology is no more or less than a *pharmakon*, to use Bernard Stiegler's term, meaning that it bears at once the potential of being poison or antidote to our contemporary condition. By condemning the digital as such we run the risk of overlooking the great potential it harbours. The problem is not digital technology, but the bad programming on which it runs today.

And this is also the general direction in which I would like to understand the discussion around the 'lack of future' we seem to be suffering from in the present. Highlighting the factual shortage of cultural, economic and technological experimentation can serve as a helpful antidote to the vacuous celebrations of changeless change washing over us on a daily basis. It would be fatal, though, if we were to extrapolate this unfortunate state of affairs to the doomsday diagnosis of a lost future. The problem we are currently confronted with has nothing to do with imperial decadence or 'living at the end times' or any such dystopian scenario.

There certainly are great challenges ahead and the neoliberal programming of our social and political infrastructure that has now lasted several decades does make it increasingly difficult to separate the future wheat from the chaffy simulations thereof. The future isn't gone; it is merely hidden behind the ideological dust constantly thrown into our eyes by the stakeholders of a social infrastructure that has become dysfunctional with regard to real innovation and progressive disruption. Today, digital technology forms a crucial part of this infrastructure, whose current bad programming prevents those 'modes of conjunction or sociability' that would generate the accidental sagacity necessary to serendipitously move into a desirable future. And it is exactly this bad programming against which this book sets out to defend serendipity.

INTRODUCTION

Structuring the Defence

The task I have set myself in this book is to mobilise the notion of serendipity in a number of ways in order to *think through* some of the popular discourses and practices that, while obsessively articulating a longing for the difference of a real future, seem to do very little to get us out of the deadlock of celebrated repetition. Serendipity, I believe, provides us with an important lead in the search for a radical politics of innovation that could, perhaps, overcome this blockage. As the accidental sagacity that has always been part and parcel of invention and discovery, serendipity reminds us of the truly *disruptive* – again, speaking strictly in the non-Californian sense of the term – dimension that has been lost in contemporary discourses on creativity and innovation. This kind of disruption is different both in kind and scale from, say, Silicon Valley's mockery of 'making the world a better place'. Instead of encouraging 'innovators', 'change makers' or 'pioneers' to feel good about what Naomi Klein aptly calls "changeless change",[18] this book intends to mobilise serendipity's disruptive potential in an effort to inflate at least some of the happy-go-lucky rhetoric

18   Naomi Klein defines changeless change as "the kind of innovation that simultaneously upends current practices and studiously protects existing wealth and power inequities." She makes this comment in her endorsement of Nicole Aschoff's (2015) *The New Prophets of Capital*, an interesting (if slightly orthodox in its academic Marxist position) book that engages with the sense and nonsense of the 'change' initiatives launched by Sheryl Sandberg, John Mackey, Oprah Winfrey, and Bill and Melinda Gates.

and adjacent practice that pass today for innovation, transformation, radical change, and so on.

In doing so, I don't expect for a moment that the notion of serendipity could serve as a semiotic panacea against the feverish stasis we seem to be trapped in. It is not my intention to provide a theory of serendipity that would 'revolutionise' our understanding of innovation or some such thing. A new concept thrown into the ginormous playground of contemporary innovation 'thinking' at best will cause a little stir in order to then be absorbed into the celebration of the innovative character of our times. Which, in fact, is exactly what is already happening. There is an expanding popular nonfiction and management literature making the connection between serendipity and business innovation.[19] One of the purposes of this publication is to show that the methods and strategies presented by these writers and entrepreneurs more or less define what a radical politics of innovation is up against today. What is at stake in this book is a defence of serendipity as a way of thinking about innovation in a political sense, i.e., as an important source of social innovation understood as a process by which a society creates the conditions of possibility for a sustainable future. Which is what I would call *A Radical Politics of Innovation*.

Serendipity lends itself to such an endeavour precisely because it goes to the heart of the question of what it means to bring something new into the world. Since Walpole's act of linguistic innovation, serendipity has been used to articulate the disruptive swerve that every act of generative *poïesis* entails. Merton and Barber's "serendipity pattern" operationalised serendipity for an analysis of scientific innovation. It is true that as a *model*, the serendipity pattern may lack the complexity and sophistication

19 To get a taste of this kind of literature see, e.g., Muller & Becker 2012, Johnson 2010, Hagel et al. 2010.

of current debates in the disciplines studying scientific practice. However, in this book, I am neither interested in the study of science nor do I intend to apply the serendipity pattern as a model. What interests me is Merton and Barber's foregrounding of accident and sagacity, because I believe that these two dimensions of serendipity provide important perspectives for an analysis of our current infrastructure of innovation, i.e., discourses, institutions, technologies, etc. that frame our thinking and practice of innovation. Therefore, this book is casually structured according to serendipity's two-dimensionality. The first four chapters look at serendipity slightly more from the point of view of *accident*, while chapters five to seven have a similar inclination toward *sagacity*. The distinction is free of analytical precision, as accident cannot do without sagacity and *vice versa*. Yet, as a shift in perspective and analytical emphasis it provides the book with the mild structure even serendipity needs.

Part 1: Accident

With regard to the problem of accident, particularly in the context of innovation, one cannot avoid reference to Paul Virilio. Over the course of the last few decades, the French philosopher has written a number of books trying to understand contemporary societies, or, as one could say, the present *conditio humana*, from the point of view of the accident. Drawing on Aristotle's distinction between *substans* and *accidens*, according to which the accident (what crops up) reveals the substance (what lies underneath),[20] Virilio argues that today we are in the grip of an ever-present threat of catastrophic accidents caused by technological accel-

20 "And so, if, for Aristotle some little time ago and for us today, *the accident reveals the substance*, this is in fact because WHAT CROPS UP (*accidens*) is a sort of analysis, a techno-analysis of WHAT IS BENEATH (*substare*) any knowledge." (Virilio 2007: 10).

eration. His argument is something like Ray Kurzweil's wacky notion of "technological singularity" in reverse: machines have already 'outsmarted' humans by way of systematic technological *Überforderung* that reveals itself in what he calls the "integral accident", i.e. the permanent and ubiquitous danger of something massively going wrong. The systematic threat of destruction puts societies into a state of shock, short-circuiting the political and economic institutions to the effect that any path to the future is blocked by fear of accident. The integral accident for Virilio is the monstrous vision that devours the social imagination and, with it, real movement. The technological singularity of society in acceleration forces us into a presentism that trades real movement for its hyperactive – and seemingly safer – simulation. As we collectively believe to be headed toward nothing but catastrophic accidents, this will be exactly where we are going.

Without wanting to embrace the dramatic techno-teleology of Virilio's thinking, I believe that the integral accident provides an important complement to the perspective of the 'lucky' accident that is said to be the linchpin of serendipity. In fact, an analysis of our contemporary infrastructures of innovation would be worthless without the lucky accident's negative other. The reason for this is simple: what connects the accidents discussed in the first part of this book is that they represent efforts motivated by the idea of fortuitous disruption (i.e., the famous lucky accident), yet only drive us closer toward the integral accident Virilio has in mind.

This is true for the so-called *creative industries*, a British-born policy that tries to structurally reform the European economy in the name of 'creative innovation' but has achieved very much the opposite. By putting culture and the arts into the straightjacket of 'valorisation' while throwing creative labour into precarity, creative industries policies have caused a major accident in the creative infrastructure of our societies (Chapter 1).

A similar logic applies to the even more recent field of *social*

33

innovation. Developed out of the correctly perceived vacuum left by the neoliberal neglect of public infrastructure, a bureaucratically managed neo-tribal activism is in the process of formation here that runs the danger of institutionalising a society-wide program of changeless change. While it was initially based on very carelessly composed conceptualities, social innovation today increasingly ossifies in a full flung ideological practice, producing endless chains of pointless accidents, also known as prototypes, that disappear as quickly as they are presented at the nearest TED-like conference (Chapter 2).

The closest we get to an 'integral accident' proper (in Virilio's sense), however, is the contemporary organisation of labour *per se*. Today, the corporate approach to 'human resource' (mirrored increasingly by public institutions) is characterised by a rather perfidious contradiction: while human resource management never tires to appeal to the creative self-mobilisation of the employee, the workforce is simultaneously pressed ever deeper into the structures of automated systems that ensure that nothing of this kind is ever going to happen. Unfortunately, the widely propagated exodus of organised labour into serendipitously creative entrepreneurship does not in any way represent a valid alternative to the Digital Taylorism of the organisation. Entrepreneurial 'liberation' tends to presuppose one's entanglement into a tightly woven mesh of technologies of the self that format individuation processes along the narrowly defined parameters of the very same Digital Taylorism the entrepreneurial renegade was trying to escape in the first place (Chapter 3).

Finally, *digital technology*, while playing an important role in all three of the aforementioned fields, merits an independent analysis as well; not so much in the sense of Virilio's dramatic showdown *per se* but rather, again, in terms of posing the question of how our thinking about technology systematically trips over what the American journalist and writer Erik Davis calls "techgnosis", i.e., the continuing entanglement of modern technoculture with myth, magic, and spirituality (Chapter 4).

Part 2: Sagacity

The second part of the book then turns to the question of sagacity. As I have pointed out above, sagacity as the second dimension of serendipity can best be understood in terms of *resistance*. When I say resistance, I don't intend it either in the sense of an act of pure defiance (like, say, Bartleby's "I'd prefer not to") or as the romantic rejection of the movement of the world motivated by the dream of an ideal past. Rather, I would like to approach sagacity as a kind of resistance that engages with the potentially new in such a way as to open up ruling regimes of knowledge and power to the possibility of future deviation. Such an understanding of sagacity takes its cue from British philosopher Howard Caygill, particularly his work *On Resistance*. In his analysis of modern theory and practice of resistance against State violence – from Clausewitz to Ghandi and Mao through to the Zapatistas, Tahir Square and Occupy – Caygill develops an ethics of resistance according to which the goal of defiance is not so much the overthrow of the powers that be but rather *the creation of conditions that ensure the survival of resistance or enhance the capacity to resist in the future*. In other words, at the ethical core of resistance, as Caygill understands it, we find the will to open up space for future deviation.

Obviously in the present context we are not dealing with State violence as such as our object of resistance, but rather with a state in which the future is violently drowned in the constant chatter about innovation. In this situation, it seems to me that we should understand sagacity in terms of the creation of conditions allowing the potentially disruptive to resist against its subsumption under ruling regimes of ideology and practice. In this sense, sagacity could be defined as the antithesis to futurology and trend watching: instead of extrapolating the future as a linear progression of trends in the current 'system', sagacity is that which intervenes as a wilful disturbance, opening said 'system' to different possibilities.

It may be surprising that, if we look at the emergence of the so-called digital revolution, we discover that the greatly innovative drive that produced the digital *pharmakon* we have to deal with today was predicated on two developments that were initially attempts at sagacious resistance: *cybernetic research* as scientific resistance against Fascism and later, in the 1960s, when cybernetics had become a weapon in the Cold War, the *counterculture* as resistance against a society whose rationality seemed at best dehumanising and hell-bent on mutual nuclear annihilation. When these two movements converged in the Seventies and Eighties, what came together were two developments that could unfold their immense innovative powers only because they were, at their very core, cultures of serendipity. This is neither to deny their enormous differences nor to ignore the fact that they both eventually failed. Yet, there are a number of lessons in this encounter of cybernetics and hippie culture that could help us to understand what sagacity, in the sense of opening space for future deviation, could mean to us today (Chapter 5).

One of the more recent effects of the 'digital revolution' is the phenomenon of the so-called *sharing economy*. Ethically charged by the explicit and implicit notion that the Internet and mobile communications enable a radical democratisation of the market, the sharing economy promises a fairer and more egalitarian capitalism through universal participation. In reality, however, the so-called sharing economy has nothing to do with sharing, equality or democracy at all. It amounts to a strategy of outright economic warfare whereby the enormous technological and financial advantage of the American military-industrial-economic complex is used in an attempt to digitally redesign our economic infrastructure according to a platform model that creates enormous wealth for owners of 'sharing' platforms while throwing its users into digital serfdom. Sagacity in this case means to see through the cheap ideological rhetoric of 'sharing' and resist the tendency towards platform capitalism in all its manifestations (Chapter 6).

In the light of the success of such perfidious attempts at ideological indoctrination, the current crisis in education, particularly higher education, is all the more worrisome. On the back of a pseudo-ethos of innovation and creative industries, a logic of 'valorisation' has all but crippled the sections of the university previously responsible for critical reflection on social processes. Again, the notion of resistance is relevant here, this time understood in terms of an educational practice of defiance against infantilisation and submission to the automatisms of market and technology. It's not a question of going back to some golden era but to rethink the university as *Übungsraum*, providing a space in which the appropriate skills can be acquired, enabling the young generation to sagaciously contribute to the economy, culture and society as such. Such a practice won't appear by itself but requires the collaboration of academics and students in an askesis of sagacious resistance, the seeds of which we are beginning to see germinate in recent university occupations (Chapter 7).

Looking over the chapters of this book, I do realise, of course, the rather defensive spirit that pervades these pages. There is a certain contradiction here, expressed already in the title of the book: *In* Defence *of Serendipity* might, in the first instance, seem to sit uneasily with *A Radical Politics of Innovation*. Yet I believe that what is really the issue with regard to a radical politics of innovation is indeed a resistance against the reckless simulations of future-mindedness that amount to nothing but the already cited changeless change. Serendipity needs to be defended as part of a political project whose goal is to undo the present so that the future can actually happen.

PART 1: ACCIDENT

I Creative Industries
Eidos between Functionalism & Dysfunction

1. Becoming Creative: A Policy Invention

Over the course of the past two decades, a strange discourse on creativity has captured an important part of cultural and economic policy. While 'creativity' is increasingly seen as a main driver of economic development, the permanent reference to creative classes, creative cities, creative innovations and so on has rendered the notion all but meaningless. Degraded to a commercial and political marketing tool, the semantic content of the notion of creativity has been reduced to a smooth flow of happy homogeneity – including the right amount of TED-styled fringe, misfits and subculture – that can be bureaucratically regulated and 'valorised'. To this rhetoric corresponds the practice of the creative industries, i.e., a radically disciplined and ordered subdomain of the economy, a domesticated creative commons where 'innovators' and 'creatives' harmoniously mingle and develop their ever-predictive 'disruptions' of self-quantification, sharing, and gamification.

How did it come to this? In Europe at least, part of this story has to do with a British policy invention that took place around the turn of the Millennium. Inspired by its less successful forerunner, the Australian Creative Nation Initiative, the British government floated the idea of the creative industries. Suddenly, creativity was recognised as something so crucial to and, apparently, pervasive in the economy that it needed to become an industrial sector. The birth certificate of this sector was issued in 1998 (upgraded in 2001) by the Blair government's Department of Culture, Media and Sport (DCMS) in the form of the so-called Task Force Mapping Document, decreeing a new post-industrial super-sector out of thirteen otherwise distinct sectors ranging from advertising and interactive leisure software to performing arts.

The central idea behind the British initiative was that in order to stay on top of the global value chain, a national economy needs to specialise in creativity and innovation. Ironically, those who had thought up this brilliant concept were a couple of former Marxist radicals, among whom Charles Leadbeater and Geoff Mulgan figured prominently. Their policy innovation was based on the assumption that the semiotic emancipation of the commodity as predicted in the philosophical writings of Jean Baudrillard or Guy Debord could actually be turned into economic policy. There is a good reason why the creative industries were invented in the UK. At that time, the British economy had already been thoroughly deindustrialised and basically deregulated to a branch of the international finance markets. In other words, it had become an economy without industry proper. Creative industries thus seemed to provide a way of keeping Britain in the economic game. It also fit the New Labour bill perfectly as creativity was neither capital nor labour in any conventional sense, instead pointing toward a third way. On top of that, Britain was assumed to be in the fortunate position of harbouring an indigenous population whose exceptional creative and innovative faculties give the country a natural competitive advantage. As Tony Blair put it: "We can say with pride that Britain is the 'design workshop of the world' – leading a creative revolution." [21]

Economically, the shift toward creativity made at least some

21   Quoted in Heartfield 2005: 18.

sense. Almost simultaneously with the launch of the creative industries meme, American business guru Joe Pine had codified the quantum leap from production to creation in his famous book, *Experience Economy*. The real products of the future economy, Pine argued, are the consumers themselves, i.e., the emotional transformation that the act of consuming a product or a service would afford in the consumer. This creation of such experiences, of course, is predicated on a much more 'artistic' understanding of business products and services than the traditional notion of production allows for.

Designers became the paradigmatic figures of the creative industries, not least because the new economic sector was supposed to consolidate those economic activities responsible for the creation of the commodities 'surface', now understood in the expanded sense of experience. And, again, these experiences were to be created rather than produced. As Diedrich Diederichsen has aptly remarked, one of the reasons why the creative industries meme caught on was its implicit promise of generating economic value as a *creatio ex nihilo*, as a quasi-magical creation out of nothing. This also presented a brilliant excuse for the neoliberal demand *vis-à-vis* artists to reinvent themselves as creative entrepreneurs. After all, artists are seen as the singular practitioners of *creatio ex nihilo*. Giving entrepreneurial artists, designers and other 'creatives' an exponential position within the economy (by granting them their own sector) was supposed to turn them into the accidental leaders of the 'creative revolution'.

The DCMS also provided the necessary data in support of the claim that the creative industries are the post-industrial economic engine: £60 billion profits in 1998 and an estimated £112 billion for 2000. Unfortunately, these numbers were largely the product of the DCMS' own creative accounting based on, among other things, the inclusion of the software industry into the creative sector. It is certainly true that by the end of the 1990s Cool

Britannia could refer to a number of achievements: Soho had just pushed Madison Avenue from the throne of the advertising industry, the Young British Artists were conquering the art world and there were a few internationally successful British pop bands. However, the phenomenon never reached a magnitude that would legitimise the belief the creative industry could lead the British economy out of its misery.

Although it failed to turn the economy into a creativity hothouse, the British initiative became a great success: as an export hit to continental policy makers. Some countries were quicker than others in adopting the approach, but today creative industries policies are a staple of European policy making. EU programs and funding schemes helped the proliferation of new government and semi-government institutions, conferences, interstate cooperation, as well as countless research and expertise platforms. EU money, of course, is always a strong incentive for policy restructuring, but I think it is fair to say that the creative industries approach caught on because it was seen by policy makers as a sensible and promising attempt to design policy tools that could effectively regulate the transition to a post-industrial economy. And so, creative policy makers all over Europe started their own creative accounting practices, showing year after year how much more 'their' sector had grown again and how, anyways, the creative industries were the real engine or flywheel – or whichever metaphor they deemed fit – of the economy. However, in the light of the on-going economic crisis it seems clear that the creative transformation was by and large wishful thinking. The economy continues to follow rationalities that are way beyond the creative forces the homonymous industries tried to summon.

And yet, there are at least two areas where creative industries policies have left their mark. One of them is surely what the British call "culture and the arts".[22] Here, creative industries policy aimed at the marketisation of the cultural sector, motivated not only by the neoliberal belief in the market but also by the idea that a greater proximity between economic and artistic rationalities would generate surprising encounters and synergies. Through creative collisions between these worlds, "culture and the arts" would become more economically sustainable, while the economy would get an infusion of serendipitous, artistic creativity.[23]

The other area of significant impact was that of creative labour. With their structural encouragement of individual entrepreneurship, creative industries policies contributed significantly to the emergence of an ever-growing network of independent (creative) professionals. The assumption here was that networks of creative entrepreneurs would create innovative ecosystems (à la Silicon Valley) and, by serendipitously colliding with companies of the established industries, would pull the entire economy into the future.

In this chapter, we are going to look at these two areas separately in order to get a sense of the achievements of the creative industries approach.

2. Becoming Functional: Culture and the Arts

Anyone who sets out to assess the impact of creative industries on culture and the arts runs into the problem that there is very little authentic data or literature on the subject. True, over the past few years we have seen a number of publications that critically engage with the movement of 'creativity' to the centre stage

22 For an interesting discussion of the shift from the 'cultural industries' to the 'creative industries', see Oakley & O'Connor 2015.
23 This theme has pervaded the creative industries discourse since its inception. For a flavour of the argument see the influential Howkins 2009.

of policy making.[24] However, while these publications often put forward important arguments against political and economic functionalisation of culture and the arts, they tend to remain at a level of theoretical abstraction that is incompatible with the discourses happening around the *realpolitik* of the creative industries. Besides, those involved in the construction of the new policy field in Britain and elsewhere don't seem all too keen to engage in a critical discussion of their practice. The idea of intercity or interregional competition, which is at the heart of the creative industries paradigm, doesn't help spread a critical ethos among public institutions. Always wary of one's brand value *vis-à-vis* supposed competitors, creative industries officials prefer to work with docile consultants and professional researchers who deliver the expected positive outlook. At the same time, universities have a hard time adjusting their programs to the interdisciplinary challenges that come with the new topologies of creative labour and entrepreneurship. Increasingly commercialised funding structures, often under the aegis of creative industries policies themselves, have all but destroyed the crucial function of the humanities and social sciences: to critically reflect on on-going social processes. All of which puts us in the unfortunate situation of having a newly established policy field without being able to properly assess it.

Given this regrettable state of affairs, Robert Hewison's

24   To get an impression of this kind of literature, see for instance Gerald Raunig's *Critique of Creativity* (2011), Andreas Reckwitz's *Erfindung der Kreativität* (2012), Geert Lovink and Ned Rossiter's *MyCreativity Reader* (2007), James Heartfield's early *Creative Gap* (2005). Guardian economists Larry Elliot and Dan Atkinson's entertaining polemic *Fantasy Island* and Owen Hatherley's *Guide to the New Ruins of Great Britain* (2010) are examples for a very critical engagement with different aspects of creative industries policy. And one should not, of course, forget renegade geographer Jamie Peck's tireless attacks on Richard Florida and the urban policies his theses instigated (see, e.g., Peck 2005).

recently published research on the development of creative industries policy *vis-à-vis* culture and the arts in the country responsible for its invention represents a first and wonderful exception. His *Cultural Capital: The Rise and Fall of Creative Britain* is a comprehensive account of the complex motivations and processes that led to the emergence of the creative industries out of the spirit of New Labour and its further development under the following Conservative-Liberal Democrat coalition government. As the title indicates, this is a book about cultural capital, and more specifically the changing political attitude towards culture and the arts.

Hewison understands cultural capital in refreshingly non-Bourdieusian terms as a form of wealth or value that, although it can be enjoyed individually, "is a mutual creation that uses the resources of shared traditions and the collective imagination to generate a public, not a private, good".[25] However, creative industries policy approaches cultural capital and its articulations in the cultural and artistic sector in rather different terms. As the author shows, the emergence of the creative industries paradigm marks a transformation in the policy toward culture and the arts that "seeks to privatize this shared wealth, absorbing it into the circulation of commodities, and putting it to instrumental use".[26] This signals a shift in policy orientation toward a rigorous understanding of culture in terms of cultural capitalism that Hewison substantiates by taking us to the backstage of Cool Britannia. As he ushers us through the transformation of the Department of National Heritage into the Department for Culture, Media and Sport (DCMS), the restructuration of the Arts Council, the formation of new agencies such as Nesta (previously NESTA, and before that known by its longer title, the National Endowment for Science, Technology and the Arts), the appointment of task

25 Hewison 2014: 7.
26 Ibid.

forces, the reallocation of budgets, and so on, the mechanics of creative industries policy become palpable. What happened – first in Britain and then with some delay on the continent as well – was the introduction of so-called "New Public Management", which meant that "the discipline and values of the market were applied to the formerly impersonal, politically and socially neutral, world of public service".[27] The whole of government – and with it the government of culture and the arts – would be restructured along the lines of business practice, or rather, its governmental simulation.

Fundamental for this process was the assumption that culture not only meant something to the economy but in fact should be seen as one of its drivers. The positive effect of the idea that culture creates wealth was that under New Labour's rule between 1997 and 2010, government spending on the arts nearly doubled. The entry charges to all national museums and galleries were removed, raising the annual number of visits from twenty-four million to forty million. Generally speaking, Britain's cultural infrastructure was improved not least thanks to the National Lottery's transformation into an engine of urban regeneration. The film industry was flourishing, regional theatres, the Royal Shakespeare Company and the National Theatre were rejuvenated and had great visitor numbers.

Yet, all this came at a price. While the idea of culture driving the economy provided a great argument for increasing arts funding, it also meant that cultural policy became besieged on two fronts: on the one hand the logic of the market, that increasingly saw cultural policy as an extension of economic policy; on the other hand the instrumentalisation of arts and culture in the government's quests for diversity and against social exclusion. Both were articulations of New Labour's populist third way renovation, while

27 Ibid.: 16.

46

in many ways also continuing Thatcherite ideologies (entrepreneurship, etc.) as well as anticipating Cameron's euphemistic Big Society. As Hewison summarises this highly ambivalent development: "culture became more 'democratic', but the democracy was the unequal democracy of the marketplace".[28]

3. Becoming Dysfunctional: From *Eidos* to Service

This is certainly true. However, the market is not the only problem here. Let's come back to Hewison's seemingly simple remark on cultural capital as "a mutual creation that uses the resources of shared traditions and the collective imagination to generate a public, not a private, good".[29] Although I believe that the use of the term 'capital' in 'cultural capital' is confusing – for isn't the notion of cultural capital trying to express a quality of relation that is explicitly different from capital? – Hewison uses it to point to a mechanism that is crucial for what we might call social (and indeed cultural) reproduction. There is an extremely interesting circularity in Hewison's statement: cultural capital is a "*mutual* creation", it "uses the resources of *shared* traditions and *collective* imagination" in order to create a "*public* good" that goes back into the process of "*mutual* creation", etc. *ad infinitum*. The process of cultural capital that Hewison describes is one that feeds off itself, precisely because it remains an open process: mutual – shared – collective – public – mutual.... What comes out of it needs to be able to go back into it again. This is the virtuously generative circularity, constantly recreating that which simultaneously belongs to all and nobody. If Hewison prefers to call it cultural capital, fine, but essentially it describes the process of culture as one that constantly regenerates an important source of social cohesion.

28 Ibid.: 33.
29 See above, FN 25.

Now, social cohesion has, of course, been one of the objectives of creative industries policies as well. Community arts, as well as other forms of instrumentalising the arts to solve social challenges locally, have become an important instrument in the toolbox of the Big Society and its continental versions such as the Dutch *participatiemaatschappij*. These can be effective tools to facilitate communities and collective action around specific problems. The proposition sounds seductively convincing: rather than having culture as something abstract in the background, let's switch to a more concrete and hands-on approach in order to solve social problems where they are actually happening. Artistic practice is approached here as direct action in the service of the social good which, again, can work just as art can be put in the service of economic rationality, as organisations such as the Swedish TILT have shown.

The moment this logic becomes problematic is when the arts – or those parts of artistic practice that are unable to survive off the arts market – are seen as valuable *only if* they explicitly serve social and political goals. The paradox is that as soon as culture and the arts are forced to work in the service of social cohesion, they lose the ability to do exactly that. The virtuously generative circularity that previously constituted a space wherein a society was able to communicate with itself in an open process, generating, in the words of Gilles Deleuze and Félix Guattari, new "affects and percepts" [30], i.e., new ways of feeling and experiencing, is disrupted by the introduction of external rationalities. What makes this so difficult to articulate, let alone defend, is the *abstract and virtual character* of the space opened by culture and the arts for the creative conversation every society needs in order to survive and, indeed, move forward. This is not to idealise culture and the arts as somehow pure and/or autonomous fields of social practice.

30   Deleuze and Guattari 1994.

48

They have always been contested by and entangled with commercial, political and other motivations. The difference today is that under the aegis of creative industries policy it becomes increasingly unthinkable that culture and the arts could do anything *but* serve society and economy in a linear, direct way. "In the past, art meant to paint pictures and make sculptures but today, artists intervene in society in a much more comprehensive way by going into organisations, communities, even factories in order to creatively change things..." is something that I have heard many times in expert circles and advisory boards for the creative industries. The danger is that we get used to the idea that culture and the arts can be used to take care of all kinds of problems, while forgetting that they themselves require our care for the sake of their very existence.

It might be interesting to note in this context that in Europe, neoliberal thinking emerged in the post-war period as the realisation that the market is not the natural phenomenon that Adam Smith thought it to be (the invisible hand, etc.) but an *eidos*; a fragile principle that needs massive care by the State in order to function at all.[31] What our current neoliberal enthusiast of all things creative industries tend to forget is that society itself – understood as the modern project of collective solidarity on a scale that exceeds the immediate sphere of community – is an *eidos* as well. Unless we want to follow cynical 'realists' such as Margret Thatcher or Bruno Latour who tell us that "there is no such thing as society", we need to engage in taking care of the *eidos* that society in fact is. And this requires a constant remaking of a public space in which culture and the arts, among other things, are able to thrive in their own right. The virtuous circle Hewison describes in the above quote demonstrates exactly the creative logic by which

31 The French philosopher Michel Foucault develops this argument in the late 1970s in his analysis of neoliberal thought. See Foucault 2008.

the *eidos* of society is actualised. By treating culture and the arts exclusively as instruments of economic and political reform, creative industries policies have at least been complicit with – if not drivers of – a process that preys on one of the essential resources society requires for its perpetual regeneration.

But let's come back to the British situation. Hewison's report from the UK is so fascinating because it reveals the deep ambivalences of creative industries policies in the country that is responsible for their invention, not least because they have been reproduced – in similar shape or form – in most of the countries that adopted them. Most importantly, it shows that economic and social lead objectives and targets make neither for sensible nor effective instruments in the area of cultural policy. With regard to the DCMS' perhaps most important lead objectives – social inclusion and audience diversity – the numbers of even the most celebratory reports remain underwhelming.[32]

The same applies to attempts at using cultural investment for the sake of economic development. In spite of the continuing flood of euphoric reports by the hired hands of not-so-independent expert institutions, the continental situation is absolutely comparable. There is, of course, a relation between culture and the economy but, a least with regard to the area of traditionally subsidised culture and the arts, it is much less linear than policy makers like to assume. As Hewison puts it succinctly in his conclusion:

> The conversion of culture into an instrument of social and
> economic policy has changed what should be an offering into a
> requirement, and a response into an obligation. But creativity
> cannot be commanded, any more than its consequences can be

32 While numbers of visitors increased, the policy goal was to change their composition in terms of race and class, which didn't happen.

predicted. Creativity depends on taking risks; the corollary is that the risk-taker must be trusted to understand the risk being taken. Everything that was done by New Labour to tie the arts and heritage into an instrumental agenda limited the creativity that it sought to encourage.[33]

There is a crucial mistake at the heart of creative industries policy: that the increasingly aesthetic, immaterial and cultural character of economic goods and services would make it sensible to regard culture and the arts primarily in terms of their economic value. This, of course, is not only neoliberal, it's also plain wrong. The incapability to distinguish between culture as capital (market) and culture as value (public realm) has caused a most regrettable policy confusion within the field of creative industries. And while the international cast of incompetent policy makers, along with their experts and consultants, carry some responsibility for the obstinacy with which this policy nonsense is perpetuated, the award for instigating this confusion goes to New Labour's ideologists. It might be interesting to note in this context that the very same confused thinkers who are responsible for the creation of the conceptual and practical mess of the 'creative industries' have since moved on to repeat their questionable magic on new policy shores. Geoff Mulgan and Charles Leadbeater, two figures who played extremely crucial roles in formulating creative industries 'thinking' in Britain, have become prominent visionaries (and in the case of Mulgan indeed an institutionalised leader) of the so-called social innovation movement. We are going to look at the theory and practice of social innovation more closely in the next chapter. As this newly emerging policy field is now spreading throughout the continent in a fashion similar to its creative predecessor, perhaps we can also take the British experience with the

33 Hewison 2014: 232.

creative industries as a warning against the uncritical imitation of British policy fashions.

4. Becoming Free: Creative Labour

Another area on which creative industries policies have left their mark is creative labour. It is obvious that the creative industries approach, with its sub-discourses such as the creative city, has done a lot in terms of managing the changing composition of the workforce. Thanks to the waves of economic crises, automation and financialisation, corporate and public organisations are increasingly unable and unwilling to absorb the masses of even highly qualified workers into their structures of employment. Simultaneously, the democratisation of digital hardware and software offered to a new generation of young, computer savvy professionals are a way of avoiding the increasingly inhospitable techno-bureaucracy of big organisations. Encouraged not least by the mystical success stories of Silicon Valleys, Alleys and Round-abouts, turning yourself into a start-up seemed to provide an emancipative alternative to the creativity-stifling, hierarchical structures of old capitalism.

Co-working spaces, creative hubs and maker labs are prolif-erating throughout the urban centres, forming a network epito-mizing the notion of the creative city. These are the paradigmatic spaces for young entrepreneurs that are emblematic for what Richard Florida famously called the "creative class". While the Creative City 101 approach, propagated by the likes of Florida and Charles Landry – build a spectacular museum and a cultural cluster and your city will thrive – had, where it didn't fail entirely, at best delivered rising real estate prices, creative industries and city policies did help to make room for a new constituency of independent, creative professionals outside the conventional organisations. In this sense, these policies enabled something of an exodus at least from the structures of industrial capitalism. Although the coworkers, creatives and makers were not quite the revolutionaries that the radical theories of exodus wanted them to be, they clearly represented a reaction to the digitally ossified structures of command and control organisations had adopted. And the same wave of digital innovation that played an important part in forcing people out of organisational structures also seemed to enable, at least formally, a more autonomous and perhaps even radical form of entrepreneurship.[34]

The downside of this development was perhaps best articulated in the notion of the "social factory" put forward by Italian post-Marxist thinkers[35] inspired to no small degree by Gilles Deleuze's remarks on the end of the "disciplinary society",[36] that signalled a leaking out of power from the institutions that, according to Michel Foucault (as well as Max Weber, Karl Marx, and many others), had contained them during the modern era. In terms of creative labour, or indeed, *potentia*,[37] an important locus of its exploitation became the urban landscape in which the majority of the population now dwelled. The social factory thesis represented, as it were, the radical theoretical analogue to the creative city, arguing that the city as such had been turned into a site of economic value creation *per se*. In the creative city as social factory, exploitation was now outsourced to the individual and often precarious members of the creative class themselves. This allowed for a hip revitalisation of the old 'entrepreneurship' meme that had been popular in the Eighties as well as the instru-

34 I'll return to the question of entrepreneurship in Chapter 3.
35 The arguments have been summarised by Gill & Pratt 2008.
36 Deleuze 1995.
37 In Italian post-Marxist theory, there is an important distinction between the power to create, i.e., *potentia* (German: *Vermögen*, French: *puissance*) and the power to dominate, i.e., *potestas* (German: *Macht*, French: *pouvoir*). See, e.g., Negri 1991.

mentalisation of the creative entrepreneurs for the sake of urban gentrification.

At the time, the paradox of liberated entrepreneurial creativity and its recapture within the social factory's conditions of enhanced precarity was a theme of hot debate also among the so-called "digital bohemians"[38] themselves. Particularly in the continental version of the coworking movement that I became quite intensively involved with, one would find not only business hipsters but also anarchists, hippies and all sorts of people who wanted "something different" to happen. It was this mixture of diverse people and motivations that gave the coworking movement its temporary edge, producing successful businesses as well as providing space – coworking spaces – where strategies against precarity were plotted and developed. Serendipity, of course, was a crucial element in these strategies: in order to survive economically they needed an environment offering a high probability of accidental encounters as a way of compensating for the freelancers' lack of organisational support structure. The groups and communities spurring the first generation coworking spaces intended to generate an imperfect yet more exciting replacement of the conventional organisation: they were supposed to generate ideas and opportunities for business, but also had a political ambition in the sense of strengthening the position of the precarious entrepreneur *vis-à-vis* potential clients through exchange of knowledge and skills, and a general practice of mutual generosity. For them, accidental sagacity provided a strategic toolbox with which to innovate their way out of the structure of employment. Their exodus, at least initially, followed the ethos: "If you want us to become neoliberal entrepreneurs of ourselves, we are going to do it on our own terms."

The establishment of this ambivalent space for the entrepre-

38 The term is taken from Friebe & Lobo 2006.

neurial exodus into the serendipitous precarity of the creative city represented a comprehensive exercise in socio-economic innovation. In macro-economic terms, the most significant effect of creative industries policy consisted not so much in the consolidation of a supposedly new economic sector but in the creation of a laboratory for social experimentation beyond the traditional structures of industrial capitalism. In economic terms, it helped to establish the practice of what Nigel Thrift called the "general outsourcing"[39] of those services that could be more effectively (and cheaply) provided by the multitude of creative entrepreneurs populating the open social factory. Big companies and organisations could now rely on a highly competitive network of independent creatives that were supported by government programs providing micro-loans, business coaching, subsidised workspace and similar infrastructural feats. Today, these programs have been complimented by a plethora of commercial offerings, nurturing the dream – and often delusion – of sustainable professional autonomy for the (more or less creative) masses.

It has often been remarked that the transformation of a significant part of the workforce into independent, creative labour results in excessive demands being explicitly and implicitly placed on the shoulders of the members of the thus constituted creative class. Besides the fact that individual economic success depends on the constant, passionate work of self-transformation and optimisation, the creative class is also expected to be the source of innovative solutions for a wide range of social, cultural and economic challenges. I have already mentioned urban regeneration, but there are much more comprehensive expectations: making national economies future-proof through technological and artistic inventiveness, democratising capitalism in the context of the so-called sharing economy, solving wicked global problems by

39   Thrift 2006: 282.

engaging in so-called social innovation, counteracting the despotic tendencies of big data and smart city technologies through design solutions for "smart citizenship" – to mention just some of the more prominent demands.

It is true that these external expectations often correspond to the (over)ambitions that are virulent within the creative class itself. In their self-perception, creative professionals often see themselves not just as entrepreneurs who want to do a good job but as "innovators", "change-makers" or "pioneers" who are here to "change the world". While the rhetoric of world-changing might for a good part be due to a mixture of self-marketing and self-delusion, it would be all too easy to entirely dismiss these tendencies as millennial narcissism. Rather, the notion of radical economic and social change through creative entrepreneurship is something that has been carefully crafted by the ideologues of the creativity discourse in order to capture the often genuine drive for change among the young generation.

5. Becoming Fed Up: Creativity Has Left the Building

Partly, this expansion of the creative industries discourse into the fluffy realm of 'making the world a better place' can be understood as the result of a survival strategy of creative policy advisors and bureaucrats. As it has become increasingly clear that decreeing a creative sector into economic being is no effective substitute for sensible economic policy, the sizeable administrative apparatus that had formed around creative industries needed new themes with which to justify its existence. One of the great sources of inspiration for the bureaucrats, project managers, consultants and experts in question was Silicon Valley's enormous media machine. That "never-drying well of shoddy concepts and dubious paradigms—from wiki-everything to i-something, from e-nothing to open-anything"[40] was more than ready to come to the aid of its European admirers. What helped was that they were rubbing shoulders anyway with the high priests of corporate world-changing on the beaten track of the 'creative innovation' conference-circus. In the hands of the creative nomenclature, the corporate slogans produced by the Silicon Valley media machine – sharing economy, big data, smart cities, social innovation 2.0, government 3.0, industry 4.0, and so on – are becoming the bottom-up tools for creative change in Europe. The reason why this works so well is that the titbits of the Californian Ideology are beautifully compatible both upward and downward.

Upward, it works because the creative industries policy makers and administrative officials sitting on the relevant funds are susceptible to the corporate coolness of many of the new topics (which they had encountered on their recent field trip to Silicon Valley anyway). Also, creative industries 'expertise' had always fed off the element of magic – after all, the image of economic value as *creatio ex nihilo* was one of its initial selling points – and now the elements of the magical brew simply receive a digital upgrade. And digital policy makers and bureaucrats do understand to the extent that it allows them to represent themselves as forward thinking and innovative.

Downward, it works because the re-launch of creative industries as "digital change for a better world" provides a platform for the plethora of nascent activist initiatives and start-ups that have emerged in the diverse areas now subsumed under the updated policy field. Ostensibly, this platform provides a public space upon which progressive, bottom-up initiatives of all stripes can serendipitously mingle, reinforcing each other and scaling their efforts in order to eventually jump over the threshold of "systemic change".

40 Morozov 2013b.

On the face of it, the idea of creating a policy platform bundling progressive initiatives with the intention to make the world a better place and support them with an adjacent institutional network is at least interesting. There are conferences, network meetings, hackathons, design camps and so on – all with the goal of mobilising and consolidating social forces for positive change. And anyway, isn't it about time that a more democratic and bottom-up structure was facilitated in Europe, providing a practical alternative to the digital dystopia international corporate interests are otherwise inflicting on us? Could this, perhaps, even be the space where the future we are missing so much is serendipitously reborn?

One of the questions we need to ask ourselves is why we should trust a rebranded network of official and semi-official institutions whose effect on culture and the arts was somewhere between ambivalent and disastrous, and that has economically, more than anything else, perpetuated the neoliberal outsourcing of creativity into the precarity of the social factory. The problem here is not so much that policy makers and their 'experts' haven't done their job well – although often they haven't – but that the job description in itself was wrong. Creative industries policies, as I have said above, represented a first attempt to react to those social, economic and cultural transformations that we associate with the immaterialisation (increasingly we reductively speak of digitisation) of products and productive processes. It is high time we admit that this attempt failed. There has been no creative transformation, certainly not of our economies. Instead, these policies have helped accelerate the demise of culture and the arts as well as the deterioration of the creative labour market. Overall, this has substantially stifled society's generative, creative capacities. Therefore, we have to stop this nonsense; the sooner the better.

II Social Innovation
The Logic of Changeless Change

1. Social Innovation: A Pudding in Need of Some Nailing

'Social innovation' is a bit of a puzzle. As a discourse it emerged out of the context of trend research and futurology driven by the conviction that the great challenges our societies are facing require new methods and strategies of renewal. Over the course of the last decade, the field of practices that understand themselves in terms of social innovation has experienced rapid growth. Increasingly, social innovation has become an important reference for national and European policy programs that address questions of 'sustainability', as well as challenges in the fields of, for instance, education, health care or social work.

One of the problems of social innovation is that it lacks a proper definition. It is a fairly incoherent body of knowledge and practices held together by the vague notion of 'making the world a better place'. Programmatic publications such as the influential *Open Book of Social Innovation*[41], and its more local offshoots[42], have not changed this situation in any substantial way. Indeed, there seems to be a widening hiatus between the increasingly grandiose claims as to the capabilities of social innovation (from solving so-called 'wicked' social problems such as world poverty or pollution to the idea of instigating 'systemic change') and the

41 Murray et al. 2010.
42 E.g., Van Abel et al. 2011.

ability to come up with a clear analytical explication of what it is one is actually doing.

Acknowledging this lack of definition is not just an exercise in academic nit-picking. The proponents of this new form of organised social activism effectively claim to have found tools and methods that can supplement, if not replace, agonistic politics as the mechanism for shaping society's future. This should be enough to warrant a request for self-reflection and analytical zeal. We simply need to know what it is we are doing when doing social innovation. Yet, a closer look at the growing social innovation scene – its organisations, conferences, publications and web forums – leads to the impression that its foundation amounts to no more than a therapeutic belief in the 'goodness' of one's action. Given what is at stake in social innovation, this is clearly not enough.

Geoff Mulgan, head of Nesta and British mastermind of social innovation, has repeatedly argued that one should not get hung up on questions of definition. Social innovation is a relatively new and evolving field of social practice, which is to say that at the moment, it might be more important to 'do' than to 'define'. We could let Mulgan and his followers get away with this seemingly well-intentioned call to get on with it already, if we were concerned with social movements like, say, the hippies in the 1960s or the *Lebensreform* movement in the 1920s. These were bottom-up movements whose impulses for all kinds of social change and innovation happened in a radically unplanned manner and often against its original intentions and motivations. Social innovation as we understand it today is the very opposite of a bottom-up phenomenon: it is an invention by policy consultants of which Mulgan is perhaps the most visible one. Its purpose is to establish an authoritative policy field that renders the otherwise rather chaotic processes of social innovation more effective by connecting them, bundling them and, if deemed appropriate, financing them as well. The very least such a project of orchestrated social change needs to do is to lay open its motivations and objectives so they can be publicly discussed. So far, such discussion has been avoided by keeping social innovation conceptually intangible.

2. Gabriel Tarde: Social Innovation between Invention and Imitation

In this analytical vacuum, German sociologists Jürgen Howaldt, Ralf Kopp and Michael Schwarz have recently intervened with a rather inconspicuous publication that for the first time makes a serious effort to develop a conceptual foundation for the practice of social innovation. One of the great things about their book, titled *On the Theory of Social Innovation* (original: *Zur Theorie Sozialer Innovationen*), is that while the authors are absolutely sympathetic to the intentions of social innovation, their attempt to cast it into a coherent analytical frame reveals some fairly fundamental limitations in its actual discourse and practices.

Perhaps surprisingly, the central reference for their theoretical effort at building a theory of social innovation is Gabriel Tarde's micro-sociology of invention and imitation. Although highly influential during his life, Tarde's thought had been eradicated from academic memory until very recently. This almost perfect erasure has to do with the fact that Tarde's work preceded the constitution of French sociology by his great intellectual adversary Émile Durkheim. Durkheim, the later father of French sociology, based the new academic discipline on what he called "social facts", i.e., "manners of acting, thinking and feeling external to the individual which are invested with a coercive power by virtue of which they exercise control over him".[43] Tarde also has a strong

43 Durkheim 1982: 52.

notion of social facts, yet the way he conceptualises them can be read as an inversion of Durkheim's sociology. Tarde's facts are social precisely because they are not imposed on the individual, but rather emerge through the individual. For Durkheim, the social is external and coercive to the individual as political animal, whereas for Tarde the social is "internal" or immanent to the individual. In fact, Tarde understands human beings (but also objects) as "micro-societies", in the sense of them being composed of a multitude of infinitesimal forces.

If this sounds rather psychological or even metaphysical for a sociologist, this is exactly why Durkheim so violently rejected Tarde's version of sociology. Tarde was interested in the micro-forces, the affects, beliefs and desires that constitute and drive society. His sociology conceptualises them as sub- or pre-individual forces and analyses how they dynamically constitute individual subjects as well as social processes. In this sense, Tarde's thought sits rather uneasily with what we have come to understand as sociology. Hence, he has been banished to "the prestigious but irrelevant position of a mere 'precursor' – and not a very good one at that, since he had been forever branded with the sin of 'psychologism' and 'spiritualism'".[44]

What makes a late-19th and early-20th century renegade sociologist highly relevant for the development of an analytically sound concept of social innovation is the fact that his sociology is at its very core a theory of innovation. However, rather than talking about innovation *per se*, Tarde approaches the issue through its conceptual neighbours, *invention* and *imitation*. According to Tarde, these are the two constitutive elements of innovation that in a strange way mirror what I suggested to be the two dimensions of serendipity: accident and sagacity. Through inventions, novelty enters into the world and it often does so – as the history of

44 Latour 2002: 117.

inventions and discoveries shows – by way of fortuitous accidents. Inventions thus form the material and the driver of the process of social change. Yet inventions become innovations only by way of imitation. An invention makes, as it were, an offer of novelty to the process of imitation. This is to say that inventions have to be picked up by a significant part of the population in order to acquire social significance, i.e., become a social fact. Tarde in this context speaks of "imitation-rays", which might be a more appropriate concept than, say, Richard Dawkins' notion of "memes", as it avoids the reductive understanding of an innovative impulse in terms of a discrete unit that is simply copied by imitation. Imitation, and I will come back to this shortly, is never *simply* repetition, but always includes the possibility of reconfiguration as well. In other words, unless there is no room for accidental sagacity to intervene, imitation is always also variation.

Conceptualising the dynamics of society as predicated on the interplay of forces on the micro level enables us to move beyond the simplistic notion of *trends* understood as passage from one particular social state to another. Instead, social change can be understood as a non-deterministic reality in its own right. For Tarde, this reality of social innovation always involves the interplay between invention and imitation. Invention and imitation are the two basic elements of his theory of innovation. Together, they form the basic social principle upon which all innovation rests.

Tarde's work thus entails a more complex and dynamic understanding of society than classical sociology: instead of the (relatively obvious) *description* of social macro phenomena (Durkheim's social facts), he is interested in the *explication* of their constitutive micro-phenomena. "[I]t is social changes", Tarde says, "that must be caught in the act and examined in great detail in order to understand social states."[45] These social changes are

45 Quoted in Alliez 2004: 52.

brought about by the interplay of invention and imitation. It is of great importance in this context to emphasise that invention and imitation are not strictly separated categories. Tarde's sociology does by no means correspond to the popular belief in heroic inventors who 'disrupt' the otherwise harmonic flow of social processes. It is true that Tarde sees in imitative repetition the basic principle of society. However, this imitative repetition is always subject to small modifications and reconfigurations. What's more, even the inventions themselves are not conceptualised by Tarde as singular events, but are the outcome of combinations or alterations of previous ideas or inventions. "With Tarde", Howaldt and his colleagues write, "inventive adaptation and disruption of imitation-rays is by no means a rare or eruptive phenomenon."[46] Rather, and here they provide a wonderful cascade of quotes from Tarde's *Social Laws*, it is

> petty, individual revolts against the accepted ethics, or through petty, individual additions to the precepts of the dominant ethics, 'minute accretions of image-laden expressions... due to some personal initiative, imitated by first one and then another', 'out of a seeming nothingness,—whence all reality emerges in an inexhaustible stream'. 'Imitation, which socialises the individual, also perpetuates good ideas from every source, and in the process of perpetuating them brings them together and makes them fertile'.[47]

Although the micro-forces that send imitation-rays through society vary to a great extent, Tarde believes that they can be grouped into two categories: belief [*croyance*] and desire [*désir*]. This is to say that the inventive imitation-rays are propagated, inhibited

46 Howaldt et al. 2014: 36.
47 Ibid.

or altered on the basis of them being either convincing/unconvincing or desirable/undesirable for the individuals through which they pass on the way to becoming social facts (or failing to do so). I would suggest ignoring, for the current purpose, the complex philosophical argument with which Tarde develops these two basic social forces on the basis of a reinterpretation of the German philosopher Gottfried Wilhelm Leibniz's monadology.[48] What is important in the present context is the fact that Tarde's concentration on these micro-forces as drivers of social processes enables him to anticipate the idea of society as a network of brains, or, indeed, a social brain.[49] Invention and imitation form the double-mechanism on whose basis social knowledge can be stored and transmitted. The 'place' of such social memory can be found, on the one hand, in the various artefacts (technologies, institutions, etc.) that have formed out of social practice and, on the other hand, in the social practices themselves.

On the basis of their rather thorough reading of Tarde, the German sociologists arrive at an initial and emphatically "non-normative" definition of social innovation, as "an intentional reconfiguration of social practices".[50] Such a definition does not exclude normative orientations and notions of socially desirable outcomes, but it doesn't presuppose them. I believe that such a cautious definition of social innovation is absolutely appropriate. Given the current conceptual confusion within the field, social innovation needs to be approached in a very careful and step-by-step manner. Let us begin to disentangle this confusion by identifying and isolating the conceptual elements that a meaningful definition of social innovation cannot take as its point of departure.

48   For a helpful discussion of this question I would suggest Eric Alliez's excellent introduction to Tarde's *Monadologie* (Alliez 1999).

49   This has been worked out in great detail by Lazzarato 2002.

50   Howaldt et al.: 13.

3. What Social Innovation is Not: Technological Innovation

The first step, I think, would be to distinguish social innovation from the currently dominant understanding of innovation that highlights its technological aspects. Tarde is indeed helpful here, as he shows the limits of technological reductionism by emphasising that "the richness (and specificity) of modern societies cannot be represented by a maximised number of artefacts and technologies".[51] While the fact that technological artefacts are always embedded in a network of social practices is a commonplace, it is one that does not seem very common among our innovation experts, researchers and policy makers. Even in the field of social innovation itself, one finds often an illegitimate equation of technology and innovation. In many cases, the understanding of social innovation is such that the 'social' in social innovation is provided by a real or imaginary social problem, while the 'innovation' part comes from the application of a new – often digital, web or social media based – piece of technology. A great example of such confused reasoning could be found for instance in Amsterdam's 2014 entry to the Bloomberg Challenge, a social innovation award tendered by New York's former mayor and media mogul. In order to innovatively respond to the challenge of rising unemployment among graduates of technical colleges, the local social innovation scene came up with an approach that targets these kids via social media, inviting them to join a gaming platform that helps them develop the right skills their schools were apparently unable to convey to them. The winners of the game are then taken into an offline coaching program and connected to great professional opportunities all over the world.

Let us ignore for the moment the fact that this smacks of a social media powered variation of *The Apprentice* and the degrad-

51 Ibid.

ing effect this would have on the students who have to game their way into a decent job opportunity. Let us also overlook the attempt at depoliticising a fundamental societal issue – caring for the younger generations – by turning it into a design challenge for software engineers. The fundamental problem lies in the carelessness with which an innovation-effort that would deserve the qualification 'social' is short-circuited here by way of a cheap digi-tech effect: "I game thus I innovate!" seems to be the motto of this project, and all else becomes secondary.

Educational games have of course long been part and parcel of modern education. Learning, at its core, is creative imitation, and play is known to be a particularly effective way of learning in this sense. And if gaming as the digitised form of play can contribute to more interesting and innovative learning environments, that's great. However, this will only be possible – and this is true for this project as much as for any other social innovation effort – if technology stops being the innovation fetish and instead is understood as something embedded in *social practices that are innovative in their own right*. I am not, of course, saying that technology should not play any or even an exponential role within the field of social innovation. It absolutely should. However, such a role would have to be defined from a very clear standpoint of what it is technology should achieve in the context of social innovation. In other words, technology needs to be qualified as a *means* of social innovation. It cannot be – and this seems to be the status of the current practice – that technology serves as a token for the innovativeness of social innovation, used to play to the policy zeitgeist in order to generate funding for ostensible 'change-making'.

Tarde's understanding of innovation is helpful here, as it exposes the reductive nature of the popular belief that the innovativeness of organisations, cities, regions or nations is a function of the number of technological artefacts they are able to generate. Tarde helps us to understand that technological artefacts are merely one dimension or element in the process of (social) innovation because they are always embedded in social practices. There can be no doubt that technological artefacts give important impulses for the emergence of new social practices. Yet, they can only do so because they have themselves emerged out of social practices in the first place. As Tarde, Howaldt & co explain, technological innovations can be described as one aspect of innovations in society that have *temporarily* become the centre of attention due to prevalent flows of invention and imitation. They represent a particular form of invention/discovery under the guise of artefacts (machines, computers, cars, etc.). This is important not just as an academic argument or refinement of a sociological theory of innovation. What this means is that whenever technologies and technological artefacts become part of the innovation game, we cannot take them at face value, we cannot understand them as innocent 'things'. From a Tardean point of view, one would have to explicitly ask for the social genealogy of the particular artefact and inquire into the "beliefs and desires" that brought it into existence. In terms of a reflexive practice of social innovation, this entails the demand of at least an awareness of economic, cultural, ideological, etc. forces that have shaped the technology one uses for one's particular purpose. In other words, the field of social innovation would gain enormously both in terms of legitimacy and efficacy by making the permanent critical analysis of the social contexts of the technologies used part and parcel of its practice. In fact, I think this would be a precondition for a timely practice of social innovation deserving of its name. The authors of *On the Theory of Social Innovation* put this very succinctly when they argue that the systematic relationship and mutual independence of social and technological innovation processes can only be grasped through consideration of the inherent laws and specifics of social innovation. This is particularly pertinent when it comes to global challenges in fields like climate change that social innovation initiatives are increasingly trying to address. As the German sociologist Harald Welzer puts it, many of the challenges we are confronted with in this area "were generated by the thoughtless application of technology in the first place. Hence, attempts to solve them by way of 'better' technologies are part of the problem and not the solution." [52]

Again, none of this is meant to demonise technology, which, of course, would be nonsensical. The point I would like to make here is that social innovation, if it wants to be emphatically *social*, cannot rely on the logic of technology. Using technology to confront a social challenge demands a critical analysis of the complexities of that challenge, as well as the technology that supposedly 'solves' it. In order to do this, social innovation simply needs to have its own distinct rationale. And no, 'making the world a better place' does not qualify.

4. What Social Innovation is Not: Entrepreneurial Innovation

Another problem that a timely definition of social innovation is confronted with is the strong economic/entrepreneurial connotation that the notion of innovation entails. Today's usage of the term seems still largely determined by Joseph Schumpeter's *Theory of Economic Development* that developed the famous notion of "creative destruction". What drives the process of creative destruction, according to Schumpeter, are innovations as successful adaptations of "new combinations of means of production".[53] As Howaldt and his colleagues aptly put it, "inventions become innovations if they are successful in the market. Introduction and implementation of innovations are the essential tasks of entrepreneurship".[54] For Schumpeter, it is the entrepreneur who

52 Welzer 2008.
53 Schumpeter 1912: 294.
54 Howaldt et al.: 29.

is the linchpin of innovation. Today, this belief in the heroism of the entrepreneur has captured once again the imagination of the innovation scene – from the most conservative policy bureaucrats to the greatest enthusiasts of social innovation. Not least the enormous popularity of 'social entrepreneurship', ostensibly defined as *doing social good by using the market as vehicle*, is testament to the strong entrepreneurial thrust in the dominant understanding of innovation in general and social innovation in particular. There is nothing wrong with this *per se* except, perhaps, for the fact that much of social entrepreneurship fails its own entrepreneurial aspirations by massively relying on sponsors and government subsidies.[55] Pioneerspost.com, an internet bulletin for the social innovation scene has recently drawn attention to this phenomenon:

> The social entrepreneur PR industry grows all the time and is hungry for content and personalities. This is dangerous and results in people being hailed as saviours and game changers when their business models are nowhere near proven – still less the damaging, unintended consequences known and understood.[56]

Social entrepreneurship promises to overcome the dualism between market and social progress. Its inventor and patron saint is Muhammad Yunus, Nobel laureate and founder of the Grameen Bank that gives micro credits to the poor in Bangladesh. People who would otherwise never receive funding for their projects get a chance to improve their lives by building a small business, etc., while the bank lives off the relatively small interest the debtors are able to pay. In the eyes of his followers, Yunus revolutionised

55 There is an excellent discussion of the friction between the ambitions and actual achievements of social entrepreneurship/innovation in the popular German business journal *Brand Eins*. See: Täubner 2013.
56 Black 2013.

the logic of development and basically single-handedly founded the practice of social entrepreneurship. The problem is that Yunus' beautifully simple idea of entrepreneurial self-empowerment does not quite live up to its promise. Even in the eyes of sympathetic observers such as David Roodman, there is no empirical evidence supporting the hype around micro-financing. In fact, the data seems to suggest that micro-finance creates more problems than it in fact solves. The reason for this is, at least in part, is as simple as Yunus' initial idea: the logic of the market cannot be suspended by the sheer force of the will to make the world a better place. The traps Yunus' approach falls into is that of Say's Law, a 19th century economics paradigm according to which "every supply creates its own demand". While Say's Law is rejected by contemporary economics across the board, applying it to the Bangladeshi poor is quite obscene: who are these new mini-businesses going to sell to? Without wanting to venture into the area of development policy, of which I don't know anything, it seems relatively obvious that for chronically impoverished parts of the world the problem is not lacking supply but rather the near nonexistence of demand. Pushing micro-entrepreneurship in these circumstances almost inevitably has the effect of intensifying competition, decreasing the market share of already existing micro-businesses and making it overall more difficult for lenders to repay their loans. So the verdict by Roodman – and again, he is a very sympathetic voice among the critics – is that on current evidence, "the average impact of microcredit on the poverty of clients is zero".[57]

The difficulties that social entrepreneurship of the Yunus kind runs into we also find elsewhere. Harmonising the logic of the market and social progress turns out to be a bit more difficult empirically than the proponents of social entrepreneurship want

57   Roodman 2012: 141.

us to believe. This isn't really surprising: there is a basic logical conflict between entrepreneurial/economic innovation and social innovation. Within the economy, the necessity to innovate is a result of the logic of competition that requires – today at increasingly shorter intervals – the introduction of new products and services (for consumption) as well as the renewal of machinery and processes (for production). While for Schumpeter, as well as for every self-respecting business man or woman, the outcome of these processes are sufficient to define progress; for the proponents of social innovation, it is not. Innovation in the economic sense is one of the major drivers of the logic of economic growth that causes many of the problems that social innovation is bent on solving. It stabilises the system rather than setting off processes leading to 'systemic change'.

There are, of course, examples where social progress and economic innovation can overlap. Yet, in order for this to happen and, more importantly, to have an understanding of when such an overlap can be defined in terms of social innovation, one first needs a robust definition of social innovation. Given that social entrepreneurship defines itself by straightforwardly invoking the Schumpeterian definition of innovation[58], it seems apposite to assume that the practice of social innovation needs to find such a definition in the first instance by keeping its distance from entrepreneurship – be it social or otherwise.

Again, I am not at all suggesting that there is anything wrong with entrepreneurial innovation. Rather, what I am suggesting is that social innovation needs to find a way to free itself from the entrepreneurial bias if it wants to distinguish itself emphatically as *social* innovation. Entrepreneurship, just as technology, can only come in as a second step, only *after* we know what we are

58   See for instance the definition by the influential Skoll Foundation, in Martin & Osber 2007.

72

doing when doing social innovation. Tarde opened an avenue for understanding social innovation that leaves the Schumpeterian entrepreneurial hero behind, instead emphasising the infinitesimal social forces of both invention and imitation that generate innovations as social facts. As Tarde writes in the concluding chapter of his *Les Lois de l'Imitation*, an innovative society is determined by the heterogeneity of the social practices it allows for. Only a society that leaves space for difference and experimentation can be a truly inventive society. With regard to our present society, it seems very important not to equate social heterogeneity with that of the market or tech-start-ups. If we look, for instance, at the history of the 'digital revolution', it is obvious to even the most mainstream commentators that the counterculture of the 1960s was absolutely instrumental to it.[59] Similarly, we know very well that in a city like Amsterdam, where I live, almost all cultural and much of the entrepreneurial innovation of the last decade has in one way or another come out of the city's lively squatting culture of the Eighties and Nineties (although it reaches much further back). The social innovation scene in its current, rather limited form, could never generate similar impulses. This is by no means a failure of those fine individuals who are working very hard to get their projects off the ground. Rather, it is a problem based on the above biases, as well as funding structures that keep the practice of social innovation locked in by heavily motivated policy programs – be they governmental or corporate.

5. Rethinking Social Innovation

So far, I have mainly referred to the problems of social innovation as a still emerging yet increasingly influential paradigm of social change. These problems, I have argued, have to do with

59 I'll come back to this question in more detail in Chapter 5.

a lack of conceptual clarity regarding what social innovation can effectively entail, what its goals are, and how they can be achieved. Taking my cue from the very helpful publication *On the Theory of Social Innovation*, I have shown that Gabriel Tarde's sociology of innovation can help us to understand that a meaningful theory and practice of social innovation can neither start from technology nor entrepreneurship. Luckily, Tarde also gives us some clues as to a timely reconceptualisation of social innovation.

According to Tarde, the only path to a meaningful notion of social innovation inevitably leads, as it were, through the notion of imitation. Imitation provides the key to understanding the emergence of novelty as a social fact in society. This might seem paradoxical, but the paradox is quickly resolved if we take into account Tarde's non-repetitive understanding of imitation that always already includes inventiveness by way of infinitesimal variations, additions, adaptations, and so on. For Tarde, imitation is the fundamental mode of social process, the 'mechanism' on which the existence of every society is based. As no society is entirely static, there must also always be – in the words of Gilles Deleuze – a difference within the repetition. What we need to take away from Tarde is the fact that it is not the great heroes – be they inventors, entrepreneurs, or indeed social innovators – who bless the repetitive rest of society with their brilliant feats. Rather, it is the multiplicity of tiny inventive imitations that at some point lead to a temporarily stabilised event to which we then assign the significance of an innovation. In the light of Tarde's own accomplishment (which, of course, is not at all his own, as he inventively imitates a multiplicity of antecedent ideas, theories, fragments), we have to contradict Isaac Newton's famous proclamation: rather than "standing on the shoulders of giants", we are surfing the waves of imitation that rise and fall according to the beliefs, desires and affects that crisscross what we call society. In other words, it is the processes of imitation themselves that go pregnant with the seeds of novelty, "like intestines in which secretly develop the types and laws of tomorrow".[60]

Understanding the emergence of novelty in society in terms of inventive imitation would imply a much more modest notion of social innovation. While it is certainly possible to give impulses for social change or try to orchestrate – in a very limited way – the multitude of inventive repetitions this should neither be equated with the idea of creative destruction nor lead to an exaggerated notion of radical, discontinuous innovation. Tarde's sociology suggests a more nuanced view of social innovation that recognises the value of existing social practices and avoids any false hopes for intentional 'change making', 'deep impact', or even 'systemic change'. Changing existing social practices implies long, contingent processes that follow their own rules, i.e., with reference to Tarde, the laws of imitation. And it is not just Tarde's theoretical explorations that lead to such a conclusion. In fact, the entire project of modern sociology bears testimony to the highly problematic nature of attempts at controlling or intentionally steering processes of social change. What policy makers and practitioners will definitely have to let go of if they want to come to a meaningful and practicable definition of social innovation, is the misconception that social change can be instigated and driven by a limited group of professional social innovators whose job is the invention and propagation of new social practices. Such an idea of intentional social change is simply nonsensical. This, I think, is not only a Tardean conclusion but also a matter of common sense. Modelling social innovation on a process of "prompts, proposals, prototypes, sustaining, scaling, systemic change" [61] illegitimately reduces the complexity of social change to the logic of successful

---

60 Tarde 1999: 80.
61 These are the steps of The Young Foundation's so-called "innovation spiral".

Internet start-ups. Luckily, society does not yet function entirely according to the logic of Silicon Valley.

Social innovation in its current form also requires a shift in perspective with regard to its ethical aspirations. It is certainly wonderful that the social innovation scene is populated by so many individuals who genuinely want to 'make the world a better place'. The question is whether the notion of innovation actually lends itself to such an ethical charge. The above discussion of the technological and economic connotations of the concept of innovation has highlighted the challenges that the use of the term innovation for ethical purposes involves. Simply putting 'social' before 'innovation' cannot solve these challenges. The perhaps unfortunate fact of the matter is that the notion of innovation is absolutely inappropriate to distinguish between 'good' and 'bad'. We have to understand that the logical difference on which innovation operates is that of old and new. It really is as simple as that. The normative nexus that the proponents of the current practice of social innovation assume ignores the ambivalence and context dependency that applies to social innovation just as much as it does to technological or entrepreneurial innovation. There is no theoretical or practical reason why social innovations should be assumed to be 'good' in the sense of being socially desirable.

Social innovations have no ethical direction. This is why there is politics. People have struggled for centuries to put in place political institutions that allow for at least a minimum of (democratically legitimated) social steering. The fact that these institutions do not function as efficiently and effectively as we would like them to, that they might even have become corrupted by anti-democratic interests, motivations and so on, does not mean that it has suddenly become possible to bypass the complexities of social life by way of intentional design processes. However, the main problem with understanding social progress in terms of designing processes that lead to ethically desirable outcomes lies not only in its lack of efficacy. In a way, the opposite is the case. We can currently observe the installation of policy programs, particularly at the European level, that adopt exactly the ethically overstrained notion of social innovation I am criticising here.[62] There is an acute danger that if such a practice becomes politically institutionalised, it is going to further support the tendency of what Evgeny Morozov in his important book *To Save Everything, Click Here* calls "solutionism". Particularly given its uncritical relation to technology and entrepreneurship, social innovation could easily turn into a grave ideological accident, cementing a practice of what Naomi Klein calls "changeless change", i.e., the kind of innovation that simultaneously upends current practices and studiously protects existing wealth and power inequities.

For those who are willing to look, there is already quite a bit of the writing on the wall in this respect. There are countless social innovation 'challenges', 'safaris', and 'retreats' whose pretentions reached from solving the Greek debt-crisis to prototyping the sustainable society. What makes these kinds of seemingly innocent attempts to try something new in the face of 'wicked' problems so dangerous is that they normalise the idea of social and potentially political activism as pure gesture. The prototype becomes the therapeutic excuse for the real political engagement without which 'making the world a better place' remains a fatal mixture of infantilism and hyperbole. And this is why we must call these pretentious change-gymnastics ideological: because they try to replace the "intestines in which secretly develop the types and laws of tomorrow" [63] with prefabricated gestures of change. If you want the world to remain as it is, this kind of social innovation is the thing to do.

---

62 A great example of this is the EU's Digital Social Innovation program. See Bria 2015.

63 Tarde 1999: 80.

6. A Radical Politics for Social Innovation?

None of this is meant to contest the enormous importance of social innovation as a political task. I wholeheartedly agree with its basic proposition that the challenges our societies are facing today can be more effectively confronted by mobilising what the Italian philosopher Maurizio Lazzarato once called *puissances de l'invention*, i.e., the social powers of invention. I also agree that we are seeing forms of social emancipation enabling citizens to more actively engage with their social environment. Beyond political opportunisms *à la* the Big Society and the like, there is indeed an innovative potential inherent in today's civil society that needs to be tapped for the transformation of the lingering institutions of industrial society. What is at stake here, as Jana Rückert-John rightly puts it, is "to enable citizens to take on a kind of responsibility for the future that is different from the individual responsibility perpetuated by neoliberal discourse".[64]

In this sense, the importance of social innovation could hardly be overstated. It would be brilliant if social innovation could grow into a practice that is modest (and honest) as to its capabilities, with less ethical hyperbole and a good portion of suspicion against the temptations of economic and technological reductionism. A promising point of departure for such a development lies in posing this important question anew: how to develop and sustain the powers of invention in our societies? Our discussion of Gabriel Tarde's sociology of inventive imitation suggests that an effective response to this question should be motivated by the desire for a maximally open and diverse society. In practical terms, this would probably entail multiple forms of advocacy for social groups and initiatives that do not fit the templates of economic or technological innovation. In such

64 Quoted in Hochwaldt et al: 66.

a scenario, social innovation would become an institution of meta-activism that works like a guardian for endangered social practices. Subcultures come to mind, but also all sorts of cultural, artistic, economic and other experiments. The focus would shift from the problematic practice of designing 'solutions' for social change – which, as we have seen above is predicated on a reductive understanding of the relationship between invention and imitation – to an approach whose goal is the facilitation of a high degree of social serendipity. And this, again, is a question of social infrastructure that can only be addressed as a political question. Instead of trying to do the impossible and establish the invention of social change as an isolated disciplinary field, social innovation could thus become part of a vision for a new society. A signpost for future orientated politics. Paradoxically, such a non-ethical reorientation would also lead social innovation to a new, more realistic and rather exciting definition of a possible ethics: that of being a counterforce to the neoliberal and technocratic tendencies of social standardisation.

III Digital Taylorism
Labour between Passion & Serendipity

1. Attack of the Big Yawn

In his fascinating historical study of the rise of happiness to the highly valued commodity it has become in our time, the British sociologist William Davies offers a brief yet intriguing meditation on the end of capitalism. In the past, he says, the collapse of our current mode of production has usually been imagined to occur as the result of economic crisis, political revolution, ecological disaster, or, in the best of cases, through technological innovation. However, since the end of the cold war, Davies muses, there seems to be another, "more lacklustre" option on the horizon:

> What if the greatest threat to capitalism, at least in the liberal West, is simply lack of enthusiasm and activity? What if, rather than inciting violence or explicit refusal, contemporary capitalism is simply met with a yawn? [65]

Williams' remarks are far less tongue-in-cheek than they may appear. There is indeed a rather telling sign of – if we were to put it in Marxist terms – capital's lack of motivational pull with regard to labour that over the last two decades has developed into a management obsession: the theory and practice of "employee engagement". Gallup started measuring employee engagement in

---

65 Williams 2015: 105.

the Eighties, its popularity as an indicator of the 'health' of a company surged in the 1990s, and today there is a plethora of refined engagement surveys and training programs available from dozens of providers. While the popularity of employee engagement is in itself suggestive of a motivational problem among the workforce – why else would one want to measure engagement? – the actual numbers these surveys regularly produce are truly disheartening for the managerial class. Gallup's last *Global Workplace Report* of 142 countries has found that only 13% of employees are properly "engaged", with those "actively disengaged" among the European and North American workforce figuring around 24%. Often, though, it's not just the ubiquitous 'yawn' ruling our corporate and public offices that is the problem. Stress-related illnesses, burnout, and similar work-induced forms of psychological and physical paralysis have joined forces to become the 21st century workspace epidemic throughout the developed world. In this sense, lack of enthusiasm or activity indeed presents a formidable challenge to our economic order, in spite of the cynical strategy to commercialise the collective disengagement by repackaging it as independent symptoms of individual psychological pathology.

What interests me in the anti-capitalist attack of the collective yawn and its pathological companions – beautifully captured by the philosopher Byung-Chul Han in the notion of the "fatigue society" (*Müdigkeitsgesellschaft*) – is that it can help us to come to terms with some of the current transformations in our understanding of labour as productive activity. In this chapter, I would like to concentrate on two developments that can be seen as attempts to respond to the challenge of the big yawn: on the one hand, the quasi-eroticisation of labour articulated in the notion of *passionate work*, and, on the other hand, the mobilisation of the social dimension of labour expressed in the celebration of entrepreneurial serendipity.

2. The Passion of the Work

While the fateful alliance between passion and labour had been anticipated by a number of visionary sociologists, such as Birger Priddat around the turn of the century, it is only recently that work is almost everywhere turning into a *passionate project*. Over the past few years, passion has become a basic requirement for employees of all stripes. Regardless of the mundane nature of the job at hand, today it is almost impossible to get anywhere near work without the invocation of one's passion for it.

As with so many of the ideological tropes discussed in this book, the connection of work and passion makes quite a bit of intuitive sense. What could be wrong with 'loving what you're doing'? If employees and entrepreneurs could be truly passionate about their work, it would turn their daily toil into a much more fun and fulfilling activity. Employers and clients, on the other hand, would profit from increased productivity and generally from a better job being done. Take, for example, one of the more authoritative publications on the topic, *The Power of Pull*, written by business consultants and management scholars John Hagel, John Seely Brown and Lang Davison. Under the heading "Make Your Passion Your Profession" they inform their readership about the new logic of passionate work:

> Those of us who continue to toil at jobs we don't love will find ourselves nonetheless toiling harder as our competition continues to intensify. We'll find it increasingly difficult to cope with the mounting stress or to put in the effort required to raise our performance. We need to marry our passions with our professions in order to reach our potential... Passion in this context refers to a sustained and deep commitment to achieving our full potential and greater capacity for self-expression in a domain that engages

us on a personal level. We often develop and explore our passions in areas such as sports or the arts outside of work, but we rarely integrate our passions with our professions.[66]

The funny thing about the logic of the argument here – and this really is a staple of the management ideology of passionate work – is that the necessity of throwing yourself passionately into the game is sold to the reader as a result of everyone being just about to do it. Maybe not today but certainly tomorrow, there will be so much passion going on in corporate and public organisations that competition becomes a question of being even more passionate than everyone else. Stress, lack of performance and cynicism are caused by insufficient alignment of one's passion to one's work. Hence, the suggested solution: get aligned, fall in love with your work already; passion is the key ingredient to professional success.

While this makes for a fascinating story, it is exactly the opposite of what a dispassionate view of reality (a.k.a. empirical data) suggests. The wave of passion that supposedly is just about to sweep through contemporary capitalism shows neither in employee engagement surveys nor in health statistics, business indicators, or macro-economic data. Nor, in fact, does it show in the great product and service innovations that surely would be the outcome of a passion-driven economy. No, the reason why passionate work has emerged as one of the great ideologies of our time is the fact that the big yawn is becoming deafening, that the neoliberal mutation of capitalism has turned the economy into a self-sabotaging system, systematically destroying its most important source of value: labour.

In order to make sense of the rise of passion to a workplace requirement within corporate and public organisations, it helps to first consider an interesting historical coincidence. The emer-

66   Hagel et al. 2010: 21.

gence of debates around employee (dis-)engagement was contemporaneous with the beginning of the systematic digitisation and automation of the workplace. In the late 1980s and throughout the 1990s, a new breed of professional service providers revolutionised the management consulting sector.[67] What they offered had very little to do with traditional board level advice. Rather, they were selling large scale IT-systems able to automate management processes throughout the entire organisation. The first wave of digitisation and automation of business came for the most part with the label of *reengineering*.[68] The grandiose claims with which reengineering firms pushed their way into corporate and public boardrooms have largely been erased from managerial memory.[69] Suffice to say that alongside predictions of increased efficiency and massively lowered costs came the promise of a workforce liberated from repetitive bureaucratic chore. Reengineering the organisation was supposed to lead to the creation of professional environments in which creativity was finally allowed to thrive.

This, of course, is not what happened. The former *Financial Times* correspondent Simon Head is one of the few scholars who have systematically traced the automation of the workplace from the *reengineering* wave of the Eighties to the current almost universal use of so-called *Computer Business Systems* (CBSs; previously known as Enterprise Systems [ES] or Enterprise Resource and Planning Systems [EPS]). His reports from the battlefield of digital armament for the sake of creatively liberated workforces

67 This shift in the consulting industry is discussed for instance in the work of Armbrüster & Kipping 2002-3, Cox & Lonsdale 1997, Kipping 2002, McKenna 2006.

68 Harris 1987.

69 The canonical text of the reengineering movement was Hammer & Champy 1993. See also Davenport & Short 1990. For an early critique from an economist's point of view see Sorge & Witteloostuijn 2004.

paint a picture of the contemporary workplace all too familiar to many of us who spend their lives within corporate and public organisations. According to Head, digitisation and automation have spread the logic of industrialism far beyond their conventional jurisdiction: to wholesale and retail, financial services, higher education, health care, public administration, and corporate management. In addition, they have also introduced the neo-disciplines of Customer Relationship Management (CRM) and Human Resource Management (HRM).

What's going on here has nothing to do with the future visions of digital machines working merrily side by side with humans. The computer systems that have been implemented throughout the economy form the technological backbone of a massive neo-bureaucratisation of corporate and public organisations. In order for the digital industrialisation of the workplace to function across different sectors, a veritable army of techno-bureaucrats has invaded corporate and public institutions whose mere task is the streamlining of employee behaviour according to the requirements of algorithmic performance indicators and the like.[70] And it is not just the infamous call centres and Amazon warehouses we are talking about here. Highly trained professionals such as doctors and professors have been pressed into preformatted work processes, effectively losing the sovereignty over their own crafts(wo)manship, expertise and knowledge. There is a systematic annihilation of professional creativity at work here, nullifying "the employee's accumulated skill, knowledge and experience which, applied to the daily problems of the workplace, enable employees to do their jobs well".[71]

---

70 For a fascinating analysis of contemporary bureaucracy from an anthropologist's point of view see Graeber 2015.

71 Head 2005: 169.

3. Faking It: Passion as Simulation

The reason why this is crucial for the present discussion is that the massive destruction of professional skill and quality by the logic of office automation was accompanied by the emergence of a new kind of competence. Arlie Hochschild famously began to describe this development in the Eighties in terms of the appearance of what she called "emotional labour". In her pioneering study of flight attendants, *The Managed Heart*, Hochschild defined emotional labour as requiring the employee "to induce or supress feeling in order to sustain the outward countenance that produces the proper state of mind in others".[72] It is obvious that thirty years ago, flight attendants' requirement to serve with a smile didn't have much to do with automation. And also today, emotional labour is not necessary directly related to CBSs and the like – although it can be if we think of the emotional stress caused by counterproductive office IT-systems. The point where digital office automation and emotional labour intersect is that of *simulation*. CBSs and their administrators are not for one bit interested in the inherent professional value of *performance* simply because they have not got the means to understand what this would actually be. They *simulate* performance by way of algorithmic indicators and matrices whose abstract universality – the fact that they need to be applicable across diverse sectors in order to be economically viable – ensures their radical decoupling from the particular professional reality (epitomised, perhaps, by the infamous star ratings for hospitals, universities and so on).

The flipside of this kind of performance *simulation* can be found in the rise emotional labour, and indeed, passion. For HRM-professionals, emotional labour is not the 'labour of care' that comes with a specific professional territory – think, for instance of phy-

72   Hochschild 1983: 7.

sicians and nurses – but the universal mobilisation of individual sources of empathy and enthusiasm for the most profane ends. The creation of *experience* as a service is an important reference here, albeit in a much more skewed sense than was intended by the gurus of the experience economy, Joe Pine and James Gilmore. In an economy where the most exciting new consumer products are digitally pimped wristwatches (first developed almost fifty years ago) and cars that actually rob you of the experience of driving, experience is something that increasingly has to be provided as a product or service veneer by the employee. The logic of the emotional template that is spreading throughout corporate and public management culture by way of HRM has been famously captured by Mike Judge's 1999 movie *Office Space*. In the film, Joanna works as a waitress in a fast food chain called Chotchkie's. An integral part of her work there is to wear idiotic buttons with slogans and symbols on them. They are referred to as "flair". At a certain point in the film, Stan, Chotchkie's manager and Joanna's boss, takes her aside in order to express his dissatisfaction with the way she's handling her "flair":

"Stan: *We need to talk about your flair.*
Joanna: *Really? I... I have fifteen pieces on. I, also...*
Stan: *Well, okay. Fifteen is the minimum, OK?*
Joanna: *OK.*
Stan: *Now, you know it's up to you whether or not you want to just do the bare minimum. Or... well, like Brian, for example, has thirty-seven pieces of flair, okay. And a terrific smile.*
Joanna: *OK. So you... you want me to wear more?*
Stan: *Look. Joanna.*
Joanna: *Yeah.*
Stan: *People can get a cheeseburger anywhere, okay? They come to Chotchkie's for the atmosphere and the attitude. OK? That's what the flair's about. It's about fun.*

Joanna: *Yeah. OK. So more then, yeah?*

Stan: *Look, we want you to express yourself, okay? Now if you feel that
the bare minimum is enough, then okay. But some people choose to
wear more and we encourage that, OK? You do want to express
yourself, don't you?*

Joanna: *Yeah, yeah.*

Stan: *OK. Great. Great. That's all I ask."*

In 1999 the scathing humour of the Judge's film was somewhat
lost in the peak of the dotcom boom, but a few years later it
became a commercial success on the small screen (VHS and DVD
sales) as a cult comment on the corporate re-entrenchment of the
post-crash years. Today, it serves as a reminder that the idiocy
expressed in the notion of "flair" has become almost universal
workplace policy. In the contemporary workplace, flair in its many
disguises has been integrated in the strange virtuosity of emotional labour. This goes for all layers of management, save the
highest, as well. Those of us who are lucky enough to be uniniti-
ated into the circuits of managerial emotional labour can begin to
bring themselves up to speed on the issue through the work of the
young German director Carmen Losmann. In her brilliant 2011
documentary *Work Hard, Play Hard*, Losmann follows a number
of so-called change management trajectories in German corporations. In one of the sequences, the viewer witnesses a series
of assessment interviews for potential junior managers who are
confronted with the most insipid questions about their emotional 'leadership qualities'. Interestingly, the candidates who do
well in the interviews are those who respond by shooting back
the prefab-slogans found on the pages of contemporary management and coaching literature. One gets the impression that what
unfolds in front of one's eyes is a grand simulation, a mutual game
of Munchausen, where everyone knows that this is essentially
nonsense but equally knows that as an employee – regardless

whether shop floor or management – one simply has to show the readiness to go the emotional extra mile. What makes this viewing experience so excruciating is the effortlessness with which the camera is able to reveal the absurdity of the change trajectories followed by Losmann's documentary. We are observers of an exercise in pointless emotional gymnastics motivated by the illusion that this will somehow vitalise corporate culture. The flair of the burger waitress returns, this time packaged in an HRM-fabricated company culture that in its ideological wackiness is easily on par with the obligatory party-gibberish that pervaded the *Kombinate* (state-owned corporations) of real existing socialism.

The obvious difference to the time of the politburo is that today, there is no central authority determining and emitting the correct world-view and watching over its implementation. Proud to be ideology-free, the neoliberal state has outsourced its ideological function – at least when it comes to labour – to the consulting industry. This is not meant as a rhetorical pun at all. If one looks at the process by which the consulting industry rose to its current dimensions, one cannot escape the realisation that it is heavily invested in the rise of neoliberal politics. The shrinking of state bureaucracy that started in the 1980s coincided with the expansion of the consulting sector that stepped in to provide the services previously run by the state itself. The reason why this worked quite beautifully was that at the same time the consulting industry underwent quite a drastic transformation – from traditional board level advice to the provision of in- or outsourced IT-systems covering the entire business process. Governments – particularly in the UK and the US – were among the first clients, providing an industry in transformation a field of large-scale experimentation by handing out consulting contracts of unprecedented financial value. The governments' benefit for subsidising and in fact growing the consulting industry was that they got the argument of technological progress to support their own ideological agenda. In other words, both the massive growth of the consulting industry in the 1980s and 1990s and the history of office digitisation and automation are intimately linked to the rise of neoliberalism.

Of course, the consulting sector is a notoriously secretive industry so much of its machinations – including the often catastrophic failures of the 1980s and 1990s IT-contracts – remain largely in the dark. It is thanks to another German documentary maker that we are able to look behind the screens of today's distributed production of ideology. In *Ein neues Produkt*, Harun Farocki follows the directors of the Quickborner Team, a Hamburg consulting firm that was once famous for the invention of the *Bürolandschaft*.[73] Today, they design corporate environments for the so-called 'new way of working', which is a big theme for corporations. In the 'new way of working', the digital automation of work processes discussed above meets the appropriation of cultural practices that independent creative producers have experimented with over the last decade or so in order to update the industrial configurations of corporate work space.

With his characteristically calm and discreet concentration, Farocki films the strategy workshops and client meetings of the Quickborner Team, capturing the semiotic dynamics at work in the development of radically innovative workplace cultures. The consultants develop the cultural tapestry for office architectures that are supposed to make employees faster, smarter, more effective and so on. The goal is flexible workspaces able to facilitate more self-determined, independent employees who, through all kinds of serendipitous interaction, contribute to the innovative capability of the company. Nothing wrong with this, let's make these environments less depressing and more interactive, if people become more productive and innovative in the process

73 For an in-depth discussion of Farocki's documentary, see Möntmann 2014.

because the new environments cater more appropriately to their professional needs, that's fine as well. Yet, what the semiotic dynamics of the meetings portrayed by Farocki reveal goes in a rather different direction. It transpires quickly that the protagonists of the film have very limited interest in understanding the needs of the 'modern employee'. The purpose of these workshops and client meetings appears to be limited to the generation of a vocabulary able to catch a managerial zeitgeist that is totally unencumbered by any substantial reflection on what flexibility, collaboration, or, indeed, self-determination might entail from an employee's point of view. Instead, the Quickborner space-gurus combine design thinking fragments, systems theory sound bites and kitchen psychology in order to produce a rhetorical vacuum that is supposed to fill their clients' workspace with what John Hagel and his colleagues call the "power of pull", attracting the passion of the employee. "It's emotionality where we can score with our clients", one of the directors of the Quickborner Team says at a decisive moment in the film, and, as silly as this may sound, he is spot on. The general ideological task of these consultants is to find the passionate antidote to the big yawn his peers have caused by implementing digital managerial industrialism.

4. Abstract Passion, Concrete Bullshit

It is obvious that nothing of this kind will ever be achieved by simply encouraging the workforce to 'fake it'. Interventions by culture consultants of the above kind are not just economically nonsensical but counterproductive. For companies that understand themselves as economic entities existing for the purpose of creating products and services that people need, they have no value whatsoever. They do, however, make perfect sense for corporations whose purpose is first and foremost to cater to the interests of financial markets. This might sound slightly vulgar

("Oh, they just want to make money!"), but it is in fact a vital distinction. One of the main reasons for the absence of exciting innovation today – increasingly even at the level of technology – has to do with what economists call "the financialisation of the economy", i.e., the fact that economic performance is increasingly measured on financial return on investment (shareholders, etc.) rather than on successful products and services.[74] Clayton Christensen, perhaps the most influential management and innovation guru of our time, denounces this tendency in *Harvard Business Review* as "The Capitalist's Dilemma". Where real economic output becomes secondary, it gets difficult to form a company culture based on the collective pride of being part of an organisation that makes great stuff. Hence the false belief in the snake oil salesmen who claim to be able to create your company/product/service culture based on hot air.

This innovation predicament is related to the neoliberal transformation of capitalism understood as the streamlining of economic production according to the needs of financial capital. The flexibility inherent to financial capital has to be reproduced at the level of the employment relation. And this is exactly the reason for the shift from professional skill to emotion and affect: the abstract liquidity of financial capital requires a corresponding liquidation of professional skill into the desires and emotional dispositions of the workforce. Today's intensified competition and chronic market instability have at least as much to do with financialisation as they do with the transformative power of digital technology. Think, for instance, of the way in which the so-called

74 There is a plethora of excellent accounts on the causes and effects of financialisation from a variety of perspectives. The most popular macroeconomic analysis with a long historical perspective is Piketty 2014. David Harvey's *A Brief History of Neoliberalism* provides a very readable contextualisation of the phenomenon from a Marxist perspective.

sharing economy is organised (see also Chapter 6). Many of the platform business models we find there are able to disrupt existing markets in spite of being economically dysfunctional. They can do this because they are highly subsidised by financial speculators whose treasure chambers are filled with capital that can't find economically sensible investment. Financial abstraction thus leads to pseudo-economic (yet very lucrative) investment games, erratic markets environments, and the need for hyperflexible employees for whom the emotional labour of passion replaces professional skill.

In such an economic environment, one can expect to find an organisational landscape that is increasingly unprepared to treat its employees like grownup professionals. There is clear evidence that working conditions have been deteriorating for years across a wide range of industries – particularly in the US and the UK. This list, provided by Simon Head, is quite comprehensive:

> [They] include increased working hours for individuals and family units; increased inequality of income and stagnant or declining real wages for a majority of the workforce; the break in the historical relationship between profits, productivity and real wage growth; loss of retirement income and shifts in the pension risk to employees, declining health care coverage and shifts of cost to employees; loss of employee voice at work as labour-movement members decline to pre-1930 levels; and increased layoffs not as a last resort but as a routine aspect of corporate restructuring. To the list should be added the increased pace of work dictated by CBSs, its intensive targeting and monitoring by 'performance evaluation' systems, and its deskilling of employees with expert systems.[75]

75 Head 2014: 118-119.

Now this is not a list cooked up by some lefty curmudgeon whose only pleasure is to critique 'the system'. It's simply a reading of mainstream statistical data on labour. Thomas Piketty, of course, wrote a bestseller based on this data, it is there for anyone who reads the newspapers, mainstream economists discuss it frequently, and anyway, we also experience these conditions on a daily basis. True, in some parts of continental Europe things are considerably less bad than elsewhere, but the tendency is a global one: there is a systematic assault on employees' ability to simply do a good job. If we correlate this development with the equally systematic requirement of employees to provide not just services but great experiences *vis-à-vis* clients and customers, a blatant contradiction comes into view. Actually, it's a double contradiction: underwhelming products and services *and* deteriorating work conditions are supposed to be balanced out by the employees' emotional labour. Time and again, they try to achieve this Sisyphean task by reaching deep into the magic box of affective human integrity in order to mobilise their emotional and communicative faculties. And if one is particularly unlucky, then one might find that all this affective energy is going into what David Graeber calls "bullshit jobs", i.e., the growing number of pseudo-professional activities that do not make a sensible contribution to society by any stretch of the imagination. No wonder everyone is yawning. Welcome to the fatigue society!

5. Exodus into Serendipity?

Given the inhospitality of office environments corporate and public, it is not very surprising that an increasing number of professionals opt out of the institutional context in order to become entrepreneurs on their own account. One form of entrepreneurial exodus, already discussed in Chapter 1, is the so-called coworking movement. When the first proper coworking spaces popped up in San Francisco, New York, Berlin and London in the early years of the new Millennium, they were born out of frustration with the confined office environment and reflected the growth of an increasingly independent workforce trying to turn their economic precarity into a neo-Bohemian entrepreneurialism.[76] Instead of the prefabricated passion of the big organisation, they were trying to get truly passionate about their profession by becoming entrepreneurs.

From the start, serendipity was an important reference for the coworking multitude: coworking spaces needed to provide their users with an environment offering a high probability of seren-dipitous encounters as a way of compensating for the freelancers' lack of organisational support structure. The groups and commu-nities spurring the first generation coworking spaces intended to generate imperfect yet more exciting replacements for the con-ventional organisation. They were supposed to generate ideas and opportunities for business, but also had a political ambi-tion in the sense of strengthening the position of the precarious entrepreneur, *vis-à-vis* potential clients, through an exchange of knowledge and skills and a general practice of mutual generosity. It is easy, too easy perhaps, to dismiss the alter-entrepreneurial euphoria of the early Millennium as a pale copy of the Californian Ideology that is now holding the start-up scene firmly in its grip. It is certainly true that the West Coast form of expression, with its endemic combination of infantile pathos and cliché, was an early visitor to the coworking community as well. Yet, underneath the silly awesomeness of everything, there was indeed awareness that it wasn't all fun and games. One of the key concerns of the early coworking movement was to help prevent the multitude

76 One of the more intellectually ambitious grassroots manifestos of this movement was Friebe & Lobo 2006. For a counter position, inspired by the work of Michel Foucault, see Lorey 2015.

of independent producers from sinking into what Byung-Chul Han calls the "solitude" of self-exploiting neoliberal subjects.[77] Here, serendipity, i.e., the accidental sagacity that emerges when people with different minds and skill sets encounter each other, was really part and parcel of the story. It turned these coworking spaces into third spaces that seemed to enable an ambivalent kind of social innovation: one that was necessary for the functioning of neoliberal capitalism but also had the ambition of going beyond it. One of the 'values' the early coworkers were passionate about was 'community', and back then this meant something more than the marketing catchphrase it has become of late. The coworking movement – or at least a substantial part of it – really thought it was possible to rewrite the rules of the neoliberal economy.

Today, coworking as a politically, culturally and even economically innovative phenomenon is all but history. The formidable spread of flex-work spaces around the globe is driven by motivations radically different from those of the early activists. Coworking has mutated into the massive provision of infrastructure for start-up entrepreneurs, independent professionals and freelancers and as such, it has become big business. Operations, such as the New York based start-up *WeWork*, are bent on turning the coworking model into a real estate version of the platform business model (see Chapter 6). Its aggressive global expansion is based on an incredible market valuation of US$10 Billion.[78] While the rhetoric of 'community' and 'values' persists as marketing strategy toward the growing client-base of independent workers and entrepreneurs in need of affordable workspace, its practical articulation has been taken over by professional hosts

77 Han 2014: 14. Han uses "solitude" in contradistinction to the famous notion of "multitude" that Antonio Negri and Michael Hardt took from Spinoza in order to mark the heterogeneous composition of the proletariat in the digital age. See, e.g., Hardt & Negri 2000.
78 Brown 2015.

and community managers. There is, of course, nothing wrong *per se* with such a professionalisation of coworking. People still need affordable workspace and flex-workspaces tend to provide exactly that. Sure, in the hands of the likes of WeWork, Regus, Liquid Spaces or indeed Marriott, coworking has lost its utopian impetus. However, if this would be all there was to it, one might bemoan it as a lost opportunity for the much-vaunted 'change', or simply write it off as the usual course of a fringe phenomenon maturing into business, and losing its more exciting, socially progressive elements along the way.

Yet, something is happening to the coworking movement that is rather unsettling. Driven by the managerial hype around serendipity – i.e., the realisation that in order to fully mobilise the workforce, individual passion needs to be complemented by the generative and, hopefully, innovative effects of social promiscuity – a growing number of smart organisation consultants have discovered coworking as a template upon which they can market their services to corporations as the new generation of change management. Again, nothing would be wrong in trying to inject the treadmill of the office with some of the serendipitous energy one sometimes encounters in coworking spaces. In fact, one would welcome this effort if it was intended as a way of humanising the corporate workspace. However, one of the obvious problems here is that coworking culture – or whatever is left of the libertarian spirit of the early digital bohemians – is very hard to decree into being in a corporate context.

6. Killing me Smartly: Serendipity in the Hyper-Taylorist Office

What is distressing about the most recent wave of coworking-inspired office reform is that its proponents seem to have something in mind that goes way beyond the superficial change gymnastics highlighted in the work of Losmann and Farocki. In a recent article in *Harvard Business Review*, three coworking visionaries/consultants are kicking off their marketing campaign for corporate coworking as a call to smart digital metrics in the name of increased 'performance' and innovation.[79] Ben Waber, Jennifer Magnolfi and Greg Lindsay are convinced that the positive effects of coworking can be realised in corporate environments if managers resort to a radically quantified understanding of serendipity:

> Few companies measure whether a space's design helps or hurts performance, but they should. They have the means. The same sensors, activity trackers, smartphones, and social networks that they eagerly foist on customers to reveal their habits and behavior can be turned inward, on employees in their work environments, to learn whether it's true that getting engineers and salespeople talking actually works.[80]

Very much like their seasoned colleagues, our new brand of innovative consultants are uninterested in substantial reflections on what collaboration, or, indeed, self-determination might entail from an employee's point of view – which is exactly what drove the early experiments in coworking. Instead, they have their eyes on the measurability of performance. Perhaps they have to approach the topic in such a way as they are trying to convince managers of the necessity of their serendipity-generating services. If one wants to land with the managerial class, one has to think like a manager. And our consultants are perfectly able to do this:

> We've already begun to collect this kind of performance data using a variety of tools, from simple network analytics to sociometric

79   Waber et al. 2014.
80   Ibid.: 70.

badges that capture interaction, communication, and location information. After deploying thousands of badges in workplaces ranging from pharmaceuticals, finance, and software companies to hospitals, we've begun to unlock the secrets of good office design in terms of density, proximity of people, and social nature. We've learned, for example, that face-to-face interactions are by far the most important activity in an office. ... [O]ur data suggest that creating collisions — chance encounters and unplanned interactions between knowledge workers, both inside and outside the organization — improves performance.[81]

While the importance of face-to-face interactions is of course anything but a secret of office design, the real innovative suggestion of our consultants here is that smart technology should be deployed to measure its impact on employee performance. What they have in mind is an office environment where a plethora of wearable technology, sensors and so on keep constant track of employees' social behaviour. The collected data are then run against employee 'performance' data. What a fantastic idea! This opens up possibilities for a radically new office culture. More than a century ago, Frederick Winslow Taylor, armed with his stopwatch, brought the principles of scientific management to the office, turning management into a highly efficient apparatus for workers' control. Today, our next generation consultants muse, the challenge lies in measuring the performance in "modern idea factories". According to them, the definition and design of the office needs to "aggressively change" from a place where work is done to a place that prescribes how it's done.

Taylorism on digital steroids! If one were to continue along this innovative line of thinking, why not throw in the instant visualisation of the social performance data as well? Surely someone

81   Ibid.: 70-71.

like the Dutch designer Daan Roosegaarde[82] could develop a ser-endipity garment that changes colour according to the number of creative collisions an employee had during a specific time period. The monthly pay cheque could become a function of the colour of your work-wear. Why not? After all we are talking about "modern idea factories", are we not?

It is, of course, rather doubtful that a wired-up workforce under permanent, meticulous surveillance is going to be a hotbed of serendipity. One really needs to have an absurdly naïve understanding of human interaction to assume that the massive deployment of smart technology for the sake of performance surveillance won't have a detrimental impact on the casual social climate everyone has known to be vital for serendipitous encoun-ters since the invention of the watercooler. But this is merely a technical point. The real scandal here lies in the exploitation of the image of coworking for the purpose of selling the idea of the office as digital control room for high-performance social interac-tion. A taste of things to come is offered by Las Vegas' Downtown Project, where Zappos is investing $350 million in the area around the company's new headquarters, which is the former city hall. Cocreated by one of our coworking visionaries, it has turned part of a Las Vegas inner-city area into a pseudo-coworking area that looks like a humongous McDonald's playground. The punch line here is that Zappos turned this part of the city into a large-scale social experiment, controlled by the newly invented metric of "collisionable hours". Their goal is "to reach 100.000 collisionable hours per acre in the neighbourhood – about 2.3 per square foot per year".[83]

82 Roosegaarde acquired regional fame a few years ago with the creation of a garment that changes its transparency depending on the frequency of one's heartbeat.
83 Ibid.: 77. For a critical assessment of the project see, e.g., Marshall 2014.

What is remarkable about this development is the breath-taking speed with which an initially quite progressive idea – to create a more humane, social and exciting work environment – has been turned into a marketing tool for hyper-Taylorist behaviour control. Within a few years, a movement with the best of intentions seems to have transformed into one of the pillars of radical corporate stasis, and even turned into a vehicle transporting the logic of digital social control out of the corporate environment into public space. Those of us who thought it possible to create a space of difference in the economy by trying to reinvent entrepreneurship have to accept that we were extraordinary naïve. Given the continuing belief in the innovative powers of micro-entrepreneurs and freelancers who tend to populate coworking spaces, it might be helpful to end this chapter by looking a bit more closely at the assumptions from which such a belief continues to be derived.

7. Anti-Serendipity: Entrepreneurship as Mobile Conformity

While the formation of today's ideology of entrepreneurialism began in the 1980s,[84] the coworking movement played a role in its consolidation in the 2000s. On the back of the digital bohemians, the notion of turning one's own existence into a passionate commercial undertaking – previously held fairly exclusively by the more radical figures within the business community, such as the legendary Tom Peters – developed into a hip and attractive proposition. Today, entrepreneurship has become something of a holy grail even for policy makers and public managers.[85] It is not only of import within the realm of the economy, but is seen as an essential subjective quality upon which the general social value

84　For a critical debate on the rise of entrepreneurialism in the 1980s see Hellas & Morris 1992.

85　Which was also prepared in the late 1980s, early 1990s as reflected by publications such as the highly influential Osborne & Gaebler 1993.

of every individual (the position one might be able to achieve within a given society) depends. Our institutions of higher education and even the curricula of our schools are redesigned as to prominently include training in the neo-discipline of entrepreneurialism that is supposed to prepare the young for the option of passionately going it alone. Part of this is motivated by a cynical realism that recognises the structural weakness of the economy, thus promoting entrepreneurial independence as a more active version of un(der)employment. The greater part of this discourse, however, is motivated by the belief that individual liberation from the hierarchical control of management is going to lead to an economic milieu characterised by free-floating entrepreneurs who – by self-organising the constant recombination of their professional passions in changing entrepreneurial networks – generate the innovative drive the big corporations are missing.

As it happens, this was almost precisely what motivated the coworking pioneers – changing the culture of corporate capitalism from a self-organised, highly innovative outside – and their story, as we have seen above, is not actually very encouraging. The fact that the euphoria for small-scale entrepreneurialism and its supposedly innovative effects on the economy is unbroken has a lot to do with a persistent misconception as to the nature of today's marketplace; particularly with regard to the capacity of markets to accommodate the proliferation of small-scale suppliers. The crucial mistake lies in the belief that thanks to the democratisation of technological infrastructure and, above all, the communicational possibilities offered by the internet, markets have become more open than ever before and are thus able to accommodate essentially an endless number of entrepreneurial offerings. The British-American writer and entrepreneur Chris Anderson presented the most prominent expression of this view in his book *The Long Tail*. Anderson argued that due to the "infinite-shelf-space" effect of online platforms like Amazon, the Internet would be able to break through the bottlenecks of broadcast and traditional bricks-and-mortar retail, thus turning the market place into an Eldorado for even the most obscure offerings (i.e., its long tail). Today's enthusiasm for entrepreneurial innovation is based on an extrapolation of Anderson thesis.

Unfortunately, even economists such as MIT's Erik Brynjolfsson, who served as one of Anderson's main witnesses for the formulation of the long tail thesis, are losing their faith in this wonderful transformation of the market. In his work with Andrew McAfee, *The Second Machine Age*, Brynjolfsson argues that the same technological developments that enable mass entrepreneurship have transformed the economic terrain into "winner-take-all markets". These are, in the words of internet critic Andrew Keen, "the opposite of Chris Anderson's profoundly flawed theory of the long tail, with its nostalgic guff on the cottage industry of middle-class cultural producers all making a reasonable living from the digital economy".[86] The long tail remains a beautiful fiction not least due to the simple fact that attention is a very scarce resource. Infinite shelves are a great thing in theory but in reality, nobody has the time, or, indeed, the attention span, to browse through them. A perfect example of this logic in the creative industries are music streaming services like Spotify and Deezer that are notoriously unviable for anyone but the absolute superstars. Add to this the hyper-exploitative platform business models of the 'sharing economy', as discussed in Chapter 6, and it becomes obvious that the level playing field upon which the increasing number of entrepreneurs are supposed to find their moderate fortunes is shrinking to say the least. Given the communicational and logistic logic of digital technology and the Internet, the super-success of the very few corresponds to the loss of the many with increasingly little in between. For those who have the

86 Keen 2015: 143.

means (and sometimes, the luck) to capture the attention of the masses, superstar status is within reach, while it becomes more and more difficult for the 'also-rans' to be even moderately successful. In the end, one simply has to admit that in its essence, the long tail is nothing but an unsuccessful attempt to resurrect (on the back of naïve assumptions as to the 'game-changing' powers of the Internet) Say's 19th century law according to which every supply automatically creates the corresponding demand. Such an endeavour might have a certain theoretical elegance to it, but it is absolutely inappropriate as a guide for today's and, indeed, future entrepreneurs.

Again, the coworking movement is a case in point here. The inability to systematically create spaces of economic difference has everything to do with the strict and narrow parameters set by today's bottleneck markets. Bottlenecks are bad for heterogeneity and difference, and we can see this reflected in the aesthetic conformity that accompanied the commercialisation of coworking. This means in turn that in terms of the physical space and workplace culture, the world of freelance entrepreneurialism has become subject to a comprehensive homogenisation that radically contradicts the notion of innovation through entrepreneurial serendipity. And it doesn't stop at spatial aesthetics. There is an army of coaches and consultants who have discovered the growing number of disoriented would-be entrepreneurs as a lucrative market. What they offer are in fact micro-versions of the services rendered by their peers in the corporate world: rhetorically embellished, off-the-shelf advice on how to be different. The ideological streamlining afforded – perhaps paradoxically – by social media also aggravates the grip of conformity even more. Given the bottleneck structure of winner-take-all markets, the initial promise of business-orientated social media – i.e., connecting the vast differences of entrepreneurial activity for the sake of unexpected, serendipitous encounters – has perverted into the provision of a near real-time scanning mechanism with which the supposed aspiring disruptors and innovators keep each other in check – and always very close to the economic zeitgeist. The rather realistic fear of not getting through the bottleneck finds its virtual expression in constant, feverish mutual adjustments that result in a mobile uniformity of epic proportions. If we were to look for serendipity here, we would find it degraded to the promiscuous construction of entrepreneurial personages: masses of desperate self-performers unified in their attempt to anticipate the right combination of boxes to be ticked in order to ride the wave of the next market fashion. Obviously, many of today's smart entrepreneurs are more than able to do this. They are performing the manic side of an increasingly bipolar economic system whose depressive dimension is represented by the big yawn echoing through public and private offices. The question is: How long is it going to take until the feverish simulation of innovation, novelty and surprise collapses under the fatigue it constantly and simultaneously coproduces? Can we really expect those whose entire professional existence takes place within the flexible template of the eternal upgrade to deliver anything but more of the same?

IV TechGnosis
Redemption *Ex Machina*

1. Accident & Techno-Mysticism

The recent popularity of Raymond Kurzweil's idea of "the techno-logical singularity" presents a bit of a conundrum. In a nutshell, it promises human salvation by Artificial Intelligence: technological singularity designates the future event at which AI supposedly becomes the *deus ex machina* of human evolution, piggybacking us into technological Nirvana. Kurzweil draws his credibility from being a famous inventor of, among other things, the first CCD flatbed scanner and the first print-to-speech reading machine for the blind. Since 2012 he is also head of Google's engineering depart-ment, where he has more or less been given *carte blanche* to turn his ideas on technological singularity and transhumanism into reality.

Kurzweil, of course, is not the first nutcase who's been lifted into the hall of ideological fame. Ayn Rand and Milton Friedman are two important predecessors whose ideas have helped to wreak the political and economic havoc we're dealing with at the moment in the form of a perpetual financial and economic crisis. The appli-cation of their ideas created a degree of desperation that, if com-bined with the threats of environmental disaster, overpopula-tion, religious fundamentalism and widespread military conflict, makes even the appeal of a utopia of *All Watched Over By Machines Of Loving Grace* (title of Adam Curtis' 2011 documentary series, borrowed from a Richard Brautigan poem) somehow plausible.

What is really worrisome, however, is the manner in which our technology elites and innovation pundits have taken on the technological singularity thesis as part of a general tendency toward techno-mysticism, substituting the utterly unfounded hope that technology itself will somehow liberate us from the necessity of critically engaging with the effects and implications of technological innovation in its current form. In this chapter, we are going to look at some of the more influential contributors to this debate, as they push the logic of serendipity to a strange and perhaps even dangerous conclusion: technological innovation in its current form might have brought us to the brink of catastrophe, but if we follow its inherent logic for just a little longer, it will produce the artificial sagacity that will save us all. Whether this logic is really going to lead to Virilio's accident of accidents remains to be seen. The question I would like to pose in this chapter is: What does it do to *our own singularity as individuals and societies*? What happens to the Enlightenment's idea of emancipation through openness in our psychic and collective becoming if the creeping conversion to techno-mysticism continues?

1. Technological Singularity

For those readers who are not acquainted with the mildly sun-stroked logic of Californian techno-evangelism, it might be helpful to briefly discuss what the notion of technological singularity entails. It is meant to describe the historical moment when human-machine interaction leads to the emergence of greater-than-human intelligence, at which point AI will follow a logic of its own thus radically changing the world as we know it. Cybernetics' *Überbrain* John von Neumann first referred to singularity in the 1950s as a potential point in the history of mankind when accelerating technological development would radically alter the mode of human existence.[87] Later, cybernetics gave rise

---

87   Von Neumann quoted in Ulam 1958: 5.

to the discipline of AI, whose long-time goal remains the machinic simulation and transgression of the human mind. Science-fiction author and AI proponent Vernor Vinge coined the notion of "technological singularity" in 1983, predicting that

> we will soon create intelligence greater than our own. [...] When this happens, human history will have reached a kind of singularity, an intellectual transition as impenetrable as the knotted space-time at the center of a black hole, and the world will pass far beyond our understanding.[88]

In his widely cited 1993 paper *The Coming Technological Singularity: How to Survive in the Post-Human Era*, Vinge predicted the advent of the technological singularity sometime in between 2005 and 2030. Due to the exponential advancement in computing by then, the technological means to create superhuman intelligence will be available to us, heralding the end of the human era. Kurzweil then took on Vinge's idea, arguing that we are approaching a point of cybernetic fusion, a point where artificial intelligence becomes so superior to its human version that it simply takes over the steering of human affairs. After that it is not only smooth but also transcendental sailing – with something like Philip K. Dick's VALIS being your friendly new cybernetic steersman.

Now, this idea of AI's benevolence is really interesting: the technological singularity has to be a radical 'game changer' if there ever was one; the end of the human era. It necessarily has to be thought as a point of total *kairos*, i.e., a point of 'pure future', when all bets are off and we're set on a path, the destination of which is totally out of our (human) hands. Nonetheless, Kurzweil and his followers somehow 'know' that after this point cybernetic benevolence will rule and we'll have things like immortality. The

88   Quoted in Brynjolfsson and McAfee 2014: 255.

more one thinks about it, the stranger this certainty becomes. Why should a dramatically superior form of artificial intelligence care about humans? Why should it attach itself to its 'creator', like Chappie, rather than simply leave the boring valley of tears like OS Samantha in *Her*? Or, indeed, why is it less likely that AI is going to do an Agent Smith or HAL on us? Be that as it may, Kurzweil's date for the arrival of artificial immortality is 2045, and he is infamous for popping an incredible amount of pills to make sure he lives to see it.

Formally speaking, Kurzweil's comeback today has to do with a careless extrapolation of something called Moore's law, which, in actuality, is not a law but an observation made in 1965 by Gordon Moore, cofounder of Intel, according to which the number of components in an integrated circuit is doubling roughly every two years (1.8 is the number usually quoted). Since this doubling of computing power has held for more than half a century,[89] it results in an exponential growth curve that is now entering the area where things are getting funky. Given that Moore's law seems also to apply to an increasing range of information technologies (data storage capacity, transmission and processing speed, microchip density), it has become a sort of master signifier within the debate on our technological future.

In order to illustrate how Moore's law is going to get us to the technological singularity, Kurzweil refers to the famous story of the invention of chess. As the legend goes, there was a very smart inventor during the 6th century CE in present day India who travelled with his invention to Pataliputra, the capital of the Gupta Empire, to present his invention to the emperor. Being overwhelmed by the beauty and complexity of the game, the ruler asked the inventor to name the reward he would like to receive

89 Just before this book went into print the 2015 *International Technology Roadmap for Semiconductors* was published, officially announcing the end of Moore's law (see ITRS 2015).

for his great work. Clever a man as he was, he answered that all he wanted was a bit of rice for his family, and since the emperor's generosity was prompted by the new game, the chessboard should be used to determine the amount of rice he was to receive. One grain on the first square, two on the second, four on the third and so on until the sixty-four squares of the chessboard are filled. Unaware of either the logic of exponential growth or Moore's law, the emperor thus agreed to give to the inventor not only more rice than he could possibly have but also more than has been produced throughout the entire history of mankind. So our inventor had outsmarted the emperor, which, it turns out, was not such a smart idea, as the ruler, for whom losing face was of course not an option, had his head chopped off. As Kurzweil puts it:

> After thirty-two squares, the emperor had given the inventor about 4 billion grains of rice. That's a reasonable quantity—about one large field's worth—and the emperor did start to take notice. But the emperor could still remain an emperor. And the inventor could still retain his head. It was as they headed into the second half of the chessboard that at least one of them got into trouble.[90]

Getting to the second half of the chessboard, in Kurzweil's view, is a metaphor for crossing the border into transhumanist cloud-cuckoo land where the merger of the human and technology bestows a goody bag on us, filled to the rim with science fiction turned benevolent reality. It is here where, as I said above, the exponential growth curve enters an area where things get funky. This – and this is what the rice and chessboard story illustrates – has to do with the fact that it is here where exponential growth gets ahead of human intuition. It is simply quite difficult to fathom the magnitude of acceleration. The problem

90 Kurzweil 1999: 36-37.

with Kurzweil's logic is of course that exponential growth in computing power, even if it migrates into other areas as well, does not in any way allow for conclusions as to the emergence of machines with autonomous intelligent capabilities that equal or even surpass the human mind. This is not to ignore the success of IBM's chess computer Deep Blue, their supercomputer Watson that knows the correct answer to almost every *Jeopardy!* question, or Google's driverless car. These are awesome technological achievements, but they remain entirely at the mercy of their programmers. They have nothing to do with cyborgs, let alone transhuman super intelligence. To extrapolate the emergence of independently living machinic intelligence – which is exactly what the singularity thesis comes down to – from improvements in computing power, processing speed and so on breaches the rules of something called logic, which is one of the great faculties of human intelligence. The proponents of the technological singularity feel quite comfortable doing so because they believe in the coming of a quasi-religious event that is going to transcend such rules. This is hocus-pocus done by Californian millionaires, and has nothing whatsoever to do with intellectual rigor at all. In fact, it doesn't even qualify as thinking.

2. Techgnosis and the Business of Anti-Enlightenment

More sober professional trend watchers and technology consultants have recently made a habit of combining Moore's law with a milder, more rational version of technological singularity as a means to scare potential clients with the unpredictable consequences of exponential technological growth. MIT business scholars Erik Brynjolfsson and Andrew McAfee provide a wonderful example of such a strategy. They use the notion of technological singularity to argue for the advent of what they announce in the title of their book as *The Second Machine Age*, i.e., an "inflection point" in the history of our economies and societies as a result of accelerating digitisation. According to the MIT professors, this is largely a good thing, bringing bounty and freedom instead of scarcity and constraint, but it will also confront us with some difficult challenges and choices.

While "inflection point" sounds much less spectacular than technological singularity, in the eyes of the two business scholars the consequences are just as dramatic. For Brynjolfsson and McAfee, things might be a bit more ambivalent than for Kurzweil, yet no less dynamic. While the exponential advancement of a wide range of computer components proves the continuing validity of Moore's law in the digital realm, the "digitization of just about everything"[91] at the very least implies an expansion of Moore's law into the 'real' world as well. "Steady exponential improvement", the two business professors state, "has brought us into the second half of the chessboard – into a time when what's come before is no longer a particularly reliable guide of what will happen next."[92] Unless, of course, one happens to be a professional futurologist or connoisseur of all things digital, in which case one can expect an exponentially growing demand for one's services. So there we go, this is the 'logic' of technological singularity all over again, but this time we at least have some MIT guys on our side to guide us through the inflection point.

Brynjolfsson and McAfee exemplify the unfortunate tendency within a certain class of academics and their trend-watching peers to turn contemporary technological innovation into a mystical force as a way of stimulating demand for their own business model as consulting exorcists. In doing so, they prey on what the American journalist and writer Erik Davis calls "techgnosis", by which he means the continuing entanglement of modern tech-

91 Brynjolfsson & McAfee 2014, Chapter 4: 57-70.
92 Ibid.: 55

noculture with myth, magic, and spirituality. As Davis shows, the enormous transformative potential that comes with new regimes of information and communication technology sparks human imagination in ways that regularly go beyond the rational. And this is not particularly surprising as these real and imagined processes of change often affect the ways in which we think of ourselves and our societies; they force us to reconsider questions of meaning, value, identity and so on. And for these questions, humans have invented (quasi-)religious institutions and tools. Hence, the current mystification of technology is not a particularly new phenomenon:

> From the moment that humans began etching grooves into ancient wizard bones to mark the cycles of the moon, the process of encoding thought and experience into a vehicle of expression has influenced the changing nature of the self. Information technology tweaks our perceptions, communicates our picture of the world to one another, and constructs remarkable and sometimes insidious forms of control over the cultural stories that shape our sense of the world. The moment we invent a significant new device for communication – talking drums, papyrus scrolls, printed books, crystal sets, computers, pagers – we partially reconstruct the self and its world, creating new opportunities (and new traps) for thought, perception, and social experience.[93]

In other words, we are not just talking about functional technologies when it comes to computers, mobile ICT, or the Internet of Things (IoT), we are talking about potentially radically transformative processes at the level of both society and self. Apparently, we as humans need the soothing or exciting power of myth to come to grips with our changing technoculture. Where

93 Davis 1998: 4.

this becomes problematic is when mythology is functionalised for the sake of stabilising existing power structures that might otherwise be challenged by the potentialities inherent within emergent technologies. And it is even more cunning when such stabilising techno-mythologies come in the guise of revolutionary thinking. This, quite obviously, has been the deeply ideological function of *Wired* magazine, particularly during the Nineties, a tradition more recently continued by TED and similar formats, whose goal is the enchantment of changeless change. Here, techno-mythology turns into the religion of big business (as well as becoming a somewhat smaller business in its own right), that today has the clear function of a networked anti-enlightenment of the 21st century.

3. Demythologising Techgnosis: Anthropogenesis as Technogenesis

That one can pay due tribute to technology's mythological dimension and still approach the challenges of technological innovation in a sincere and critical way shows in the work of French philosopher Bernard Stiegler. Myth, and more specifically, Greek mythology, is Stiegler's point of departure into a political philosophy of the present that takes on the experience of cybernetics in the sense of thinking the development of humanity and technology as one of radical co-evolution. For Stiegler, the human being is technological by nature. This is not as a result of recent technological progress, but because our intimate relationship to technology is exactly what defines us as human. The human being, he argues, is ontologically defective and needs external prostheses in order to survive and evolve. He traces this idea back to Greek philosophy, with Plato being his central witness. In the *Protagoras*, Plato lets Socrates recount the myth of the titan Epimetheus, Prometheus' slightly silly brother, who, in the process of making mortals, used the bag of attributes he could spend on the creatures (strength, speed, claws, etc.) rather unwisely, so when it was time to create a human being, there was nothing left. Thus, in order to correct his brother's fault and provide the human being with the necessary means for preservation, Prometheus had to steal from Hephaestus and Athena their technical skills, along with the use of fire for which he then had to endure his well-known punishment.

In the spirit of techgnosis, Stiegler's account takes recourse to Greek mythology, but in contradistinction to the above-discussed entrepreneurs of mystical uncertainty, he is not interested in enchanting the relationship between technology and the human. His entire philosophical project is geared toward the development of a deep understanding of the complexities of human-machine interaction, with the goal of overcoming what he believes to be today's deep crisis of this relationship. In order to find the conceptual tools for this task, he departs from the realm of myth and turns to the study of the interface between anthropogenesis and technogenesis by way of palaeoanthropology, history and, of course, philosophy. It would be futile to attempt a summary of the sophisticated argument Stiegler develops in his foundational trilogy *Technics and Time*. Suffice to say here that he arrives at an understanding of technology that doesn't reduce it to technical artefacts, but tries to capture the entire human-built environment. Technology, or, as he prefers to call it, technics, is an "associated milieu" providing human beings with the external organs needed for survival and evolution.[94] Technics, in other words, represents the "organological" infrastructure (objects, artifices, tools, but also social institutions) through which human beings relate to themselves, each other and the world, thus making us who we are in the most basic sense. Technology, one could say

94 For a more extensive explanation of technology as "associated milieu" see, e.g., Venn et al. 2007.

with Stiegler, is the way in which humans *program* the environment in order to make it inhabitable. With reference to his teacher Jacques Derrida, Stiegler calls this process of programming "grammatisation", which is to say that the infrastructural transformation (making habitable) of the world is done in writing, or at least this is how it starts (the externalisation of speech through the invention of writing), moving on to bodily gestures (industrial machinery), and finally the mind itself (from computer networks to AI).

By successively externalising its potential (which is also an internalisation of the world in the sense of infrastructure as organ), humanity invents itself by inventing technology as organology. Strictly speaking, the human doesn't exist prior to the invention of technology, which is also the invention of time and space. As I have said above, according to Stiegler, the human being is a prosthetic being in so far as s/he needs technological organs in order to survive and evolve. What is crucial here – and in a way also only logical – is that this prosthesis is at once a pro-thesis, in the sense of technology being always already ahead of humanity. It is through technology that we anticipate the future by continuously trying to resolve the problem of the originary default, i.e., the fault of Epimetheus. By way of technology, humanity articulates time and again throughout its history the Promethean rebellion against the divine authoritarianism of necessity.

Stiegler here departs from two of his major philosophical influences, namely Martin Heidegger and Edmund Husserl, who in the first half of the 20th century warned their contemporaries of the destructive force of technological rationality and scientific positivism. The apparatus erected on these principles, Husserl and Heidegger argued, is one of ontological domination, i.e., as one might put it, the radical functionalisation and determination of being for the sake of techno-scientific progress. They saw this process as so brutally reductive on being that they believed it would inevitably lead into catastrophe. The reason why such a critique sounds rather anachronistic to our ears is that it rests on a strict dualism between the human (or, indeed, being) and technology. In our cybernetic times of intensive human-machine interaction it has simply become empirically impossible to conceive of such a strict distinction.[95] And thanks to Stiegler, we can now understand that anthropogenesis and technogenesis could never be distinguished to begin with, but have to be thought in terms of the process of the evolution of life by means other than life. They are two sides of the same token that Stiegler coins "epiphylogenesis". This neologism is meant to define human-machine coevolution as a process by which the individual (and collective) experience of *epigenesis* is accumulated within the technological infrastructure, i.e., the associated milieu that Stiegler, following Simondon and Deleuze, marks with the biological notion of technological *phylum*.

What makes Stiegler's philosophy so incredibly helpful in relation to the technological singularity thesis is that it shows that singularity defines the relationship between humanity and technology from the outset. What does singularity mean as a philosophical concept? It denotes the radical openness of the process of human becoming (which, again, is always already becoming-through-technology) in ways that defy necessity, determinism, and blind repetition. Singularity is another version of the living revolt against the Gods that has been famously expressed in philosophical notions such as Spinoza's undetermined body, Marx's species being or Nietzsche's *Übermensch*. The strength of the human weakling lies in her/his ability to overcome her/his

95 As Erich Hörl (2008) has shown, Heidegger did, however, anticipate the enormous consequences the cybernetic challenge would have on the "dogmatic image of thought".

originary limitations by way of perpetual self-reinvention. Technology or technics is the milieu (the phylum in epi*phylo*genesis) through which this reinvention proceeds. Such an understanding of singularity, which, again, comes with a substantial philosophical history, refutes the notion of technological singularity on at least two counts:

First, it exposes the thesis' pleonasm because it shows that singularity with regard to human becoming has to be thought in terms of technology or cannot be thought at all. What Stiegler's analysis reveals is not only the logical nonsensicality of technological singularity but also the ideological strategy behind it, i.e., the attempt to illegitimately 'emancipate' technology from the human with the goal to turn it back into a God-given force of necessity. Technology is sold to us as an ontologically independent phenomenon to which human beings can only react.

Second, and in a similar vein, it rubbishes the idea of singularity as a future event. How could singularity be projected into the future? It is the mode of human becoming as expressed in the development of and interaction with the technological infrastructure. To project it into the future as an event of technological redemption serves only those who want to cloud humanity's awareness of its inherent openness and freedom (to become otherwise). To say that at some future date radical change will occur amounts to saying that until this date, such change is impossible. This is wrong. The singularity is not near, as Kurzweil put it some time ago, it is here and it always has been – at least as a constant potential.

4. The Accident of Neoliberal Politics: Infrastructural Degeneration

We can now understand that the technological singularity represents a form of technological mysticism that corresponds to the classical definition of ideology: a belief system that turns populations into docile followers of the dominant logic of power. The technological singularity expels the memory of Prometheus' bravery from epiphylogenesis, putting the future of humanity firmly into the hands of the idiot Epimetheus. According to Kurzweil and his following, we have simply to accept our defective mode of existence until the neutral law of technological progress pans out one way or the other.

Now, let's be clear about this: nothing in the area of digital technology 'just happens'. The technological trajectory we find ourselves on today is the result of the complex (and sometimes not so complex) interplay of financial, military and industrial interests and motivations. The reason why the 'digital revolution' is creating a plethora of wicked problems – from individual psychopathologies to economic crises and social catastrophes – does not lie in the logic of new technology *per se*. Again, Stiegler is helpful here as he approaches technology in terms of *pharmakon*, the Greek term meaning at once *poison* and *cure*. This is to say (something that should actually be commonplace): technology is never neutral or innocent; it carries within itself the potential to create wonderful things as well as be terribly destructive. If we see today that the balance is tilting toward the poisonous, this simply means that our programming is bad. And this bad programming actually has a name: neoliberal politics. I am not using the notion of neoliberalism lightly, say, as a global denunciation of 'the powers that be', but as a term to describe the incredible neglect with which our political elites have treated the question of social infrastructure in general and digital infrastructure in particular.[96] This really is the essence of neoliberal politics with regard to the 'digital revolution': the systematic refusal to take responsibility for the care (read: good programming) of society's digital infrastructure, allowing for its degeneration into an apparatus of marketing and finance. There is nothing wrong with marketing and finance *per se*, but if they become the hegemonic rationales guiding the development of technology, if they are not couched within a political project of care for the future, accident will be unavoidable. Stiegler describes this development as capitalism losing its spirit, if not, indeed, its mind – a development Max Weber already foresaw in the early 20th century.[97] A different way of putting this is to say that without the necessary political care, capitalism is without an ethical compass, which brings with it the danger of what historians of the rise of fascism like Detlev Peukert or Zygmunt Bauman have termed *Machbarkeitswahn*, i.e. a hubris that is toxic because of its inability to ask for the consequences of its actions. A frightening illustration of such *Machbarkeitswahn* we find today in the development of military AI. Stephen Hawking and more than a thousand of his colleagues in robotics and related fields have recently published an open letter desperately calling for a ban on military AI, "our biggest existential threat".[98] If the technological singularity is indeed near, it seems as if it will arrive in the guise of a very dangerous AI arms race.

However, one doesn't need to focus on the military to come across the obscene consequences of neoliberal *laissez-faire* policy with regard to our digital infrastructure. In Europe, the politi-

96 Even Rosabeth Moss Kanter, the *grande dame* of Harvard Business School has just published a book criticising the systematic neglect of infrastructure in the US as a serious social and economic problem. See Kanter 2015.

97 Stiegler 2014b. See also the closing remarks in Weber 1976.

98 See Gibbs 2015.

cal neglect of digital infrastructure has for many years been personified in the figure of Neelie Kroes, former Vice President of the European Commission. A YouTube video made in early 2014 shows Kroes giving a presentation on "healthcare in your front pocket", where she praises the advantages of electronic wristbands that monitor one's health, fitness, movements and so on.[99] In times of demographic ageing and malfunctioning health systems, these devices might or might not have great merits for those who want to get or stay healthy. The point is that Kroes acts like a salesperson for the industry rather than a political representative. As one the most powerful European politicians, why did she feel that it was her place to deliver a marketing act for devices whose use, in terms of privacy issues but also efficacy, is far from undisputed? Why did a politician of her standing publically degrade herself to a pusher of self-quantification gadgets?[100] Part of the answer, I think, lies in the fact that this kind of politics as reading out user manuals for personal management and control systems is the wet dream of neoliberal politics. It is a politics free of politics, a form of government that has degenerated into technocracy pure and simple.[101]

---

99 This video appalled the late editor of the *Frankfurter Allgemeine Zeitung*, Frank Schirrmacher, so much that he took it as an occasion to turn the paper's Feulliton section into a discussion forum on the relation between politics and the 'digital revolution' (Schirrmacher 2014).

100 The punch line to this story Uber delivered in May 2016 when the company appointed Kroes to an extremely lucrative position on its Public Policy Advisory Board.

101 Indeed, if we are to belief Yanis Varoufakis, the former Greek Minister of Finance, reading out manuals was also the only response he received from the Eurogroup in reaction to his putting forward political and economic arguments against austerity. For the time being, the neoliberal emancipation of government from politics reached its European climax in the treatment of Greece.

5. Teleology Reloaded: Revolution Ex Machina

Given the bleakness of my analysis here, one might wonder what has happened to the positive impulses the Internet and digital technology were supposed to generate. Was not the Internet once thought to be a greatly democratising force, bound to erode old hierarchies and offer unprecedented economic opportunities by granting access to markets, long tails and all the innovative rest of it? In other words, what has happened to the 'cure' side of the technological *pharmakon*. Have we lost it? Has it withered away? Or is it perhaps hiding somewhere in the shadows?

Not if one cares to talk to (or read) Jeremy Rifkin. In his latest book, *The Zero Marginal Cost Society*, he praises the revolutionary force of an emergent digital infrastructure that he sees coevolving with new forms of collectivism – both social and economic, and often at the same time. Now not only does this sound like great news, it also fits into Stiegler's philosophical model of epiphylogenesis, i.e., the evolution of humanity by way of its technological milieu. Perhaps it is Rifkin who can help us find the nexus connecting (perhaps a new form of) politics to the progressive potential of digital technology.

Rifkin's book looks indeed promising. It's not really a blockbuster title, but that doesn't mean that this would be one of Rifkin's minor books. In fact, what the American Business School academic and head of the Foundation on Economic Trends attempts here is a synthesis of the rather enormous body of work that stands to his name. From his almost prophetic book on the technology-induced decline of the global workforce (*The End of Work*) and his take on the experience economy (*The Age of Access*), to the more recent thesis about capitalism as an operational accident in the history of mankind (*The Emphatic Civilization*) and the proclamation of a *Third Industrial Revolution* based on the convergence of smart grid energy and distributed communication networks, Rifkin has emerged as one of the most influential commentators on social and economic change, and is in great demand as a policy and business consultant in Europe, particularly with the German government.

"The capitalist era is passing... not quickly but inevitably."[102] Thus reads Rifkin's opening sentence, setting the tone for an argument that imagines the end of capitalism as the result of two simultaneous "revolutions". On the one hand, there is the technological revolution, i.e., the rapid advances in digital and neo-industrial technology leading to the emergence of a lateral infrastructure for production. Rifkin subsumes this development under the metonym of the Internet of Things (IoT). On the other hand, there is the social revolution manifesting itself in cultural and economic initiatives of sharing, social innovation, and just generally a change toward more open, democratic and non-proprietary practices throughout society. At their point of intersection emerges a new singularity, a space for a new turn in the history of humanity, articulated by Rifkin's vision of a post-capitalist society. How could one not be excited about such a bold thesis? Let's see if it holds any water.

The Zero Marginal Cost Society is organised around the conceptual backbone of the IoT. While in the popular use of the notion of IoT what is usually meant is the spill over of digital networking into the world of physical objects based on the proliferation and interconnection of microprocessors and analytic software apps, Rifkin argues for an even more inclusive, all-encompassing understanding of the Internet of Things. His IoT features three dimensions: energy, communication and logistics. First, there is what he calls the "energy-internet", representing the trend toward smart grid technology, i.e., the distributed generation of renewable energy (every house as a micro-power plant feeding into the grid,

102   Rifkin 2014: 1.

etc.). Second, we have the distributed communication network, the Internet. Together, those two form what Rifkin calls the energy/communication matrix.[103] The third dimension, then, is provided by a smart and distributed logistics system that is not really here yet but according to Rifkin, trends such as ubiquitous sensors in retail automation, smart cities, big data technologies, etc. clearly point in this direction, and anyway, this simply is the way things will (have to) go.

Together, these three dimensions make up "the first general purpose technology platform in history that can potentially take large parts of the economy to near zero marginal cost".[104] Now, what does "near zero marginal cost" actually mean? In economics, marginal costs signify the investment necessary to produce one more unit of a particular good. As costs tend to decrease with increasing numbers of goods produced, over the long run, the cost of such investment becomes marginal. According to Rifkin, near zero marginal cost is the result of what he refers to as the "ultimate contradiction at the heart of capitalism",[105] i.e., the race for technological innovations lowering production costs and prices for the sake of competitive advantage. In other words, capitalists compete for customers, ergo goods and services get cheaper, ergo profits fall over time (Marx famously expounded this argument as the "tendency of the rate of profit to fall"). Today, Rifkin argues, the convergence of the energy, communications and logistics Internets on one all-encompassing IoT will, eventually, lead to the evaporation of profit for significant parts of the economy. We see this already happening in indus-

---

103   In fact, in the first chapters of the book, he attempts a rewrite of the history of capitalism (against Marx and Smith) as one driven by the co-evolution of energy and communication technologies rather than (the organisation of) labour power.

104   Ibid.: 138.

105   Ibid.: 70.

tries dealing in digitised or digitisable goods (publishing, enter-tainment, etc.), but in the eyes of the futurologist, this is only the prelude to a new great transformation. With profits gone, capitalism will be eclipsed, i.e., if it won't disappear entirely, it will at least move to the margins of the economy.

A small caveat is in order at this point. There is a difference between capitalism and markets. Although capitalism has been defined in quite a few different ways over the course of modern history, it is usually described as a specific mode of production that comes with its specific mode of ownership of the means of production. Markets, on the other hand, are modes of distri-bution of goods and services. They might be seen as part and parcel of capitalism but they are not synonymous with it. As readers of the French historian Fernand Braudel might remem-ber, historically, capitalism hasn't really been all too keen on markets anyway. That this remains true today is demonstrated by the monopolistic tendencies and covert price-fixing in the technological top-sectors. And, of course, the famous high-tech investor Peter Thiel effectively claims in his book *Zero to One* that competition is for losers.

Taking the difference between capitalism and markets into account, which Rifkin doesn't, would mean to understand that the collapse of certain markets does by no means logically lead to a collapse of capitalism at all. Leaving this not so minor misun-derstanding aside for the moment, the question is: Where does the path beyond capitalism lead according to Jeremy Rifkin? The answer is the "social economy" or "Collaborative Commons", i.e., the laterally structured social system that coevolves alongside the IoT. Of course, as with the IoT, the Collaborative Commons are still emerging, but the signs, according to the author, are all over the wall: trends such as the sharing economy, free and open software initiatives, or social innovation make clear which way we are going. And while "emerging" is in fact a diplomatic way of saying that something isn't really here (yet), the prospects for the social economy are outstanding thanks to its "soulmate", the IoT:

> The new infrastructure is configured to be distributed in nature in order to facilitate collaboration and the search for new synergies, making it an ideal technological framework for advancing the social economy. The operating logic of the IoT is to optimize lateral peer production, universal access, and inclusion, the same sensibilities that are critical to the nurturing and creation of social capital in the civil society. The very purpose of the new technology platform is to encourage a sharing culture, which is what the Commons is all about. It is these design features of the IoT that bring the social Commons out of the shadows, giving it a high tech platform to become the dominant economic paradigm of the twenty-first century.[106]

What Rifkin presents is thus a dialectic where the technological advances synthesised in the notion of IoT drive a transformation of the economy to the effect that the benevolent human tendencies toward sharing and collaboration become the operating principles of a new economic order. The teleology that Rifkin developed at length in *The Emphatic Civilization* is here, put on the rails of the IoT in order to reach its final destination: socio-economic "Commonism". Whereas in the past, people believed they needed to struggle for revolution as a way of overcoming capitalism, we now know that it was simply a matter of waiting for technology to lend a hand to the course of history by bringing out the internal contradictions of a social system that will now lead to its more or less gentle self-destruction.

Suggesting the existence of such a dialectic, I think, is historically nonsensical and intellectually frivolous. However, what

106   Ibid.: 14.

makes one cringe in desperation when reading Rifkin's book is that one can't help wishing that he was right. The idea of more collaborative economic institutions within a more egalitarian society supported by the democratising potential of digital technology represents a wonderful vision of a possible future. And this, one would hope, could be the positive effect of Rifkin's writing: to popularise the idea that our digital infrastructure harbours the seeds for a different and better future. What is less helpful is his 'method' of lumping together a wide variety of often contradictory 'trends' and extrapolating them into seismic shifts toward a radically democratic, post-capitalist economy. At times, Rifkin's book reads like the work of someone who spends a good part of his life traveling from one innovation conference to the next, taking all the presented arguments at face value. 3D-printing, crowdfunding, MOOCS, driverless cars, DIY, big data, and, of course, Moore's law and technological singularity – you name it, it's in the book. And he mixes it all into a dialectic where the transformation of human society into a network of collaboration, sharing and so on is a function of a human-machine interaction that is fully determined by the sheer force of technological progress.

And this is where Rifkin's argument reveals itself as being of the same ideological order as the technological singularity thesis. To his mind, the advent of a more humane society is the result of a benign trick technology is playing on capitalism, leading to an event by which the collaborationist tendencies in society are transferred from the back seat of the economy into the driver's seat. Perhaps Rifkin really believes this is going to happen, but there isn't much empirical evidence to substantiate such a belief. His celebration of the so-called sharing economy (he uses "Collaborative Commons" synonymously) is understandable but misses the point; in Chapter 6 I am going to demonstrate that 'sharing' is no more than a camouflage term for platform business models that are commons-based only in so far as they create common misery for those who have to sell their labour on them. However, the reason why those in charge of these hyper-exploitative platforms (as well as their powerful investors) are successfully spreading throughout the world is that they can tap into an international circuit of ideology generation that constantly provides them with an arena (TED-like conferences, publications, web-forums, etc.) where the spin of sharing and collaboration is being doctored. Rifkin is one of the smoothest operators in this arena. He might be a post-capitalist revolutionary at heart, but intellectually he is a demagogue of capitalist regression, pointing back to the future of digital serfdom!

7. Political Pharmacology: Beyond the Commons

If technology is a *pharmakon* that can be either toxic or healing, then we need a politics that is willing and capable to make the difference. The crucial thing to grasp today is that the technological nature of human being comes with the obligation to care for its externalised organs, to tend to and nurture the technological infrastructure in such a manner that the future remains an open and desirable 'place'. We need to take care of our external organs; we can't risk them becoming toxic, as they then might indeed harm us. The politics of collaboration and the Commons, even those of the genuine, authentic kind, have so far not proven to be up to the task at all. On the contrary, wherever people gather in the name of the Commons, community or collaboration – as they do, for instance, in the social innovation scene (Chapter 2) – they tend to celebrate a neo-tribalism that requires constant rhetorical hubris to hide its embarrassing political weakness.

Again, I am as appreciative of Rifkin's vision of an economy on par with the collaborative and democratic potential of digital technology as I am of the techno-tribes prototyping designs for a better society. However, as long as they don't shed the belief in a technological *telos* eventually tipping the scale of power in favour of the Commons, their political efficacy will remain negligible, making them vulnerable to every kind of ideological appropriation. In fact, the techno-teleology of the Commons amounts to no more than a light version of the technological singularity. It projects a quasi-mystical event (revolutionary power shift) into an uncertain future, deflecting from the necessity of real political engagement as care for the technological organs through which humanity evolves (what Stiegler calls *epiphylogenesis*). This is the real question of the singularity, and it can only be addressed by engaging in a struggle to reclaim the imperfect political institutions we, as societies, have at our disposal today. And this, clearly, requires a reframing of the question of digital technology within a greater vision of a more democratic and egalitarian social infrastructure where the care for our externalised organs corresponds to the care for an imaginary 'we'. I am going to return to this question in more detail in the conclusion to this book. Suffice to say for now, the odds against such an endeavour are enormous. Yet history has shown time and again that they can be beaten. It's not a question of personal or tribal preference, it simply has to be done. Teleological fantasy and mythical self-deception have brought us way too close to Virilio's integral accident.

PART 2: SAGACITY

v Make Love & War
Silicon Valley's Original Sin

1. Introducing Jobs' Law

In the contemporary debates on innovation there exists a well-known phenomenon that might be described as *Jobs' Law*. It applies to conferences, symposia, and web discussion, but also to plain conversations that are somehow related to the topic of innovation: within a few minutes, Silicon Valley will have entered the discussion as a sort of yard stick by which the theory and practice of innovation have to be measured. On the face of it, this is neither surprising nor remarkable. Silicon Valley has been the geographical nexus of the last comprehensive wave of innovation whose technological, economic and cultural effects continue to determine substantial parts of our lives. So yes, of course people talk about it when talking about innovation.

The reason why the Valley-chatter is not only annoying but also troubling is that it has become a master signifier, blocking anything that may lay behind it from our view. The problem is that the digital industry for which Silicon Valley stands as a geographical metaphor has captured the imagination of our policy and decision makers to an extent bordering on the absurd. Today, nearly every official statement local politicians emit regarding the economic future of their cities and regions will necessarily involve the commitment "to become the next Silicon Valley". Of course, the incredible accumulation and concentration of wealth that resulted from the previous great wave of technological innovation has produced an industry whose power and influence is truly awesome. While the biggest players among them have financial means at their disposal that make smaller nation-states blush, their powers of public persuasion and marketing are simply unparalleled. Which leaves us with the unfortunate situation that the centre of yesterday's technological and economic innovation is able to elevate its digital entropy to the exclusive image of our global future. Apparently, the future has become an image of the West Coast past.

The interesting paradox about the widespread celebration of well-marketed digital stasis lies in the fact that it betrays even the most mainstream accounts of Silicon Valley's rise to the centre of the 'digital revolution', such as Walter Isaacson's bestseller *The Innovators*. After all, did Gordon Moore and Robert Noyce found Intel in order to recreate Fairchild? No, of course not. They wanted to break with a corporate culture that they thought had become dysfunctional to innovation. And neither did Steve Jobs try to copy IBM, the most successful ICT company at the time, when setting up Apple. He and Wozniak might not have known what exactly they were doing, but it was clear to them that they didn't try to copy anyone's 'best practice'. They weren't asking the question: "How to best repeat the past?"; they were saying: "Let's see what comes next!".

However, if we leave the dimension of popular management nonfiction for the more complex terrain of social history proper, a story presents itself that even more radically contradicts the idea of Silicon Valley being the end point of innovation history. It is this story that I would like to bring back to mind in this chapter. Its title, *Make Love & War*, refers to the encounter between the two historical trajectories that were absolutely pivotal for the emergence of the phenomenon 'Silicon Valley': the cybernetic research culture of the American military-industrial-academic complex (War), and the experimental lifestyle of Sixties hippie culture (Love). As I am going to show, each of these movements represented its own specific culture of serendipity. And when they collided in the late Sixties and early Seventies, a serendipitous event took place that proved to be decisive for the technological, economic and cultural shape of things to come in the US and beyond. The genealogy of the two cultures of serendipity, as well as their encounter, will be the subject of our investigation in the present chapter.[107]

What makes a closer look at these developments instructive is that it may shed some light on the relation between serendipity and innovation as a social process by which a given society creates the conditions of its own future. It exposes – or so I hope – the fundamental fault in the currently dominant thinking about innovation in our societies: that the future should be thought as a linear – or for the believers in 'technological singularity', an exponential – extension of the past. As the previous wave of radical, society-wide innovation gave us digital technology, computers and the Internet, we assume that innovation today is a question of merely upgrading our current operating system. This, however, is absolute nonsense. The future did not become digital in the Sixties and Seventies by projecting the past onto it. It became digital through a disruption caused by the convergence of two cultures of serendipity that imagined the future – each in their own problematic way – as a radical break with the past.

2. War & Innovation

In his afterword to *The Travels and Adventures of Serendipity*, written nearly half a century after the original manuscript, Robert

107 It will necessarily entail a cursory and somewhat fragmented presentation of events given the constraints of a single chapter. Furthermore, I am not pretending to present findings of my own original research, as this chapter is entirely based on my readings of existing literature.

Merton warns his readers of the psychological reductionism he sees at work in an understanding of serendipity that locates it in the nature or talent of a specific individual. Instead, he argues, serendipity should be approached as an emergent property of "sociocognitive microenvironments" allowing for interactions that are sufficiently undetermined with regard to both their form and their content. What Merton has in mind are environments conducive of open-ended exploration and transversal knowledge-exchange. He exemplifies such an environment with reference to Thomas Kuhn's discovery/invention of the logic of shifting scientific paradigms. Kuhn spent a number of years in academic institutions with an ethos of what Merton calls "institutionalized serendipity", meaning environments in which interdisciplinary exchange is formally and informally facilitated (such as the Harvard Society of Fellows and the Center for Advanced Study in the Behavioral Sciences in Palo Alto). As Merton is able to show, residing in such environments led to a variety of serendipitous incidents that were crucial for the formation of Kuhn's theory of scientific paradigm shifts.

It is by no means an accident that Merton is able to link Kuhn's theoretical breakthrough to the phenomenon of institutionalised serendipity. In the 1950s, the Center for Advanced Study in the Behavioral Sciences was part of a research culture that had emerged within the American military-industrial-academic complex during World War II. Perhaps somewhat ironically, this research culture was characterised by an openness and interdisciplinarity that went beyond even Merton's idea of institutionalised serendipity. The wartime research labs, as well as their cold-war successors, were instrumental in the development of the interdiscipline of cybernetics that – as is well known – laid the scientific foundations for the invention of the computer as well as the so-called digital revolution.

One of the first instantiations of institutionalised serendipity in Merton's sense emerged in the 1940s at the Radiation Laboratory (Rad Lab) at the Massachusetts Institute of Technology (MIT). As an integral part of the military-industrial-academic complex, the Rad Lab was instrumental in the development of computing. It was also one of the places from where Operations Research (OR) was launched in the US. Initially a British invention, OR became the systematic effort of integrating the natural sciences (and later social sciences and economics) into the military apparatus as a science of war. It entailed the practice of bringing theoretical scientists into the field to design wartime technologies in collaboration with the usual engineers. And yet, the abduction of science for military purposes was less of a linear process that one might expect, creating, perhaps paradoxically, institutional spaces for unprecedented interdisciplinarity. For the Rad Lab, as an early experiment in OR, this meant that scientists and mathematicians from MIT and elsewhere worked together with engineers and designers from different industries, as well as many different military and government planners. As Fred Turner shows in his brilliantly informative *From Counterculture to Cyberculture*, the Rad Lab was a place of intense collaboration and independent thinking. It was also a place where specialist scientists were encouraged to cross over to other fields in order to be able to design and build new technologies. And in the spirit of OR, scientists and engineers had to think logistically as well, assembling networks of technologists, funders, and administrators in order to realise their projects. As Turner writes:

> Neither scientists nor administrators could stay walled off from one another in their offices and laboratories; throughout the Rad Lab, and even after hours, in the restaurants and living rooms of

Cambridge, the pressure to produce new technologies to fight the
war drove formerly specialised scientists and engineers to cross
professional boundaries, to routinely mix work with pleasure,
and form new, interdisciplinary networks within which to work
and live.[108]

Such a description of the Rad Lab has a surprisingly contemporary ring to it; comprising many of the elements that today are
seen as essential for any institution operating within the sphere
of the 'knowledge economy', 'creative industries' or, indeed,
'innovation'. For Turner, the Rad Lab exemplifies the development of early 20th century structures of institutionalised serendipity in the context of the "forgotten openness of the closed
world" of war- and later Cold-War-related research. However, the
formal organisation of the nascent OR efforts alone does not tell
us much about the internal processes of knowledge creation. In
this respect, the work of the eminent historian of science, Peter
Galison, is particularly enlightening. Galison develops the notion
of the "trading zone" with particular reference to the work of the
Rad Lab, but it would probably be safe to say that it also applies
to other institutions of the military-industrial-academic complex
at the time. He derives the term from work done in anthropol-
ogy in order to understand inter-tribal communication practices.
As anthropologists know, trade is a way of enabling exchange
between groups with substantial differences in their cultural and
semiotic practices. Galison describes this as follows:

Two groups can agree on rules of exchange even if they ascribe
utterly different significance to the objects being exchanged; they
might even disagree on the meaning of the exchange process

108   Turner 2006: 19.

itself. Nonetheless, the trading partners can hammer out a *local* coordination despite vast *global* difference.[109]

It should be clear that the transversal bridging of fundamental linguistic differences is quite crucial to the generation of a serendipitous climate within sociocognitive microenvironments in Merton's sense. Galison in this context speaks less of one 'shared culture' than of different knowledge "subcultures", unified, of course, by the purpose of first, winning the war, and later on, competing with the Russians in the Cold War. The challenge for the different academic subcultures was to find the communicational means that ensured a high degree of serendipity within the trading zones.[110]

3. Cybernetic Serendipity: Collaboration & Reduction

One of the truly paradigmatic figures within the emerging practice of institutionalised serendipity was Norbert Wiener, mathematics prodigy and father of the discipline of cybernetics. Cybernetics, defined by Wiener as "the scientific study of control and communication in the animal and the machine",[111] was conceived of as a field of study and research with the purpose of describing and steering human-machine systems by means of mathematical operations (the term cybernetics derives from the Greek *kybernētēs*, steersman). As it evolved, cybernetics became a

109 Galison 1999: 138, original italics.

110 Galison's work also serves as a welcome reminder that talk about 'like-mindedness' as a 'success factor' in today's communities and groups devoted to knowledge creation, innovation and so on is no more than idle chatter. What we can learn from Galison is that when it comes to knowledge creation and veritable innovation, the potent mixture is very much characterised by unlike-mindedness in combination with a milieu/ environment facilitating transversal bridging in terms of trading zones.

111 Wiener 1961: 10.

radically transdisciplinary platform on which much of the conceptual groundwork was done that proved instrumental for the later development of computers, robotics and digital technology in general. However, while preparing the world for an extraordinary cascade of technological innovation, Wiener and his colleagues also unleashed a new way of thinking about nature, society and what it means to be human.

At the Rad Lab, cybernetics was born in the context of Wiener's work on an anti-aircraft fire-control system that could predict the movement of bombers and thus increase the effectiveness of anti-aircraft gunners. In order to get to such a predictive device, the pilots as well as the gunners had to be conceptually reduced to info-mechanical devices. As it was clear to Wiener that the human element could not be eliminated from the behaviour of the enemy, it needed to be assimilated into a system that could be mathematically represented. He needed a mechanical analogue for human behaviour in order to represent the gun pointer and pilot that he eventually found in the negative feedback loop.

In order to inscribe the "human element" into the human-machine system comprised of soldiers, planes and guns, a double reduction of the human was necessary: on the one hand, the pilot and gunner had to be understood in terms of a servomechanisms within one single system; on the other hand, they became sources of information for a feedback loop. This radically reductive understanding of human agents in terms of mechanical regulation and informational feedback is in fact what lies at the origin of cybernetics. Although Wiener failed to construct the anti-aircraft predictor, he succeeded in instigating an ontological metamorphosis that led to our current understanding of ourselves as "infomechanical beings", to use an expression introduced by Brian Holmes. Yet while Wiener and his colleagues engaged in their ontological reductionism for the purpose of winning the war, they went about it in a manner that was all too human. For

despite his brilliance, Wiener could not of course create cybernetics on his own. Rather, as Turner puts it,

> he pulled its analytical terms together by bridging multiple, if
> formerly segregated, scientific communities. Wiener borrowed
> the word *homeostasis* from the field of physiology and applied it
> to social systems; he picked up the word *feedback* from control
> engineering; and from the study of human behavior, he drew the
> concepts of learning, memory, flexibility, and purpose. Wiener
> could assemble pieces from such diverse sources because he was
> in steady collaborative contact with representatives from each of
> these domains at the Rad Lab, in his famous hallway wanderings
> at MIT, and in his sojourns to the Harvard Medical School. In the
> course of these peregrinations, he discussed physiology with
> Arthur Rosenblueth, feedback with the engineers of the Rad Lab,
> and, very likely, human behavior with both. Like the anti-aircraft
> predictor itself, the rhetoric of cybernetics was the product of
> interdisciplinary entrepreneurial work.[112]

In other words, Wiener's project, at the core of which was the
reduction of human behaviour to its info-mechanical dimension,
was itself situated in an environment facilitating forms of social
interaction that his theory necessarily had to exclude. The cybernetic reduction that, as Katherine Hayles famously put it, hinged
on the "disembodiment" of human communication, emerged in
an academic climate catering to such fuzzy qualities as intuition
and curiosity that very much define the ontology of the human
in so far as it is exactly not mechanistic or informational. It was
perhaps Wiener himself who best personified the paradox of
cybernetics. He was famous for his walks across campus at MIT
where "he was a familiar sight standing splayfoot, his cigar posed

112 Turner 2006: 24-25.

in his right hand at the level of his mouth, pouring out on student, janitor, business manager or astounded colleague witticisms or profundities of science with equal gusto".[113] Wiener was very much the ideal type of serendipitist, with all the idiosyncrasies of a human, all too human, member of the academic community. And yet, he was also the scientist who, perhaps unwillingly, led us to a way of thinking that increasingly leaves little room for human complexities of the nonlinear kind – be it in academia or elsewhere.

4. Cybernetic Serendipity: Collaboration through Reduction

However, there is yet another side to the paradox of cybernetics. While the new discipline was being constructed within an institutional culture embodying the kind of interaction the theory worked hard to erase, cybernetics itself became an important instrument for serendipitous exchange. Again, its universality hinged on the assumption that, as Hayles put, "humans and machines are brothers under the skin".[114] The canonical text that developed the equivalence of humans and machines into a kind of cybernetic metaphysics was a paper entitled "Behavior, Purpose and Teleology", written by Wiener, his long-time collaborator, the engineer Julian Bigelow, and the physiologist Arturo Rosenblueth. The conclusion drawn by the authors was that "a uniform behavioristic analysis is applicable to both machines and living organisms, regardless of the complexity of the behavior".[115] The great advantage of this inbuilt conceptual reductionism was that it turned cybernetics first into what Turner calls a "local contact language", enabling cross-disciplinary collaboration in

---

113   Barbara Wiener quoted in Conway & Siegelman 2005: 195.
114   Hayles 1999: 50.
115   Wiener et al. 1943: 22.

the war labs and later into something of a universal discipline for the coordination of research across disciplinary boundaries. The cyborg metaphysics that underlay the new meta-science paradoxically created the rhetorical apparatus for a veritable orgy of a strange kind of scientific serendipity:

> [S]pecialists in one discipline began to do things that had previously been considered the proper domain of specialists in other areas. They could justify such leaps across disciplinary boundaries by drawing on the rhetoric of cybernetics. If biological principles were at work in machines, then why shouldn't a physiologist contribute to work on computers? If 'information' was the lifeblood of automatons, human beings and societies alike, why shouldn't a mechanical engineer become a social critic.[116]

Thus, in formal terms, what cybernetics achieved was the construction of a language that could bridge different academic subcultures with unprecedented effectiveness.[117] By doing so, it unleashed an enormous wave of human creativity, eventually leading not only to the invention of the atomic bomb and, indeed, the computer, but also to the construction of a new image of the human being. An important landmark on the way to such a scientific as well as cultural achievement was a series of conferences sponsored by the Josiah Macy Jr. Foundation. Instigated not least by the above-mentioned paper by Wiener, Bigelow and Rosenblueth, the Macy conferences were essential for the estab-

---

116 Turner 2006: 25.

117 This chapter focuses on the ambivalent interdisciplinarity of cybernetics. However, as Jamie Cohen-Cole demonstrates in *The Open Mind*, values such as autonomy, openness and interdisciplinarity defined the ethos of American academic life in the post-war period (his particular focus is psychology but his discussion extends well beyond that), thus facilitating the emergence of the interdiscipline of cybernetics.

lishment and diffusion of cybernetics as a way of interdisciplinary thinking. The ten relevant conferences on cybernetics were held between 1946 and 1953. One of the reasons for their success in spreading what Philip Mirowski in his monumental *Machine Dreams* called "cyborg science" was their interdisciplinary and, indeed, serendipity-inducing set up. The list of participants includes many of the time's top academics from a wide range of fields. Besides the cybernetic pioneers like Norbert Wiener, Arturo Rosenblueth, Warren McCulloch and John von Neumann, participants included mathematicians, biologists and physicists but also big names from the social sciences and humanities such as the psychiatrist Ross Ashby, sociologist Paul Lazarsfeld, or the anthropologists Gregory Bateson and Margaret Mead. Yet, their success was for a good part also predicated on their unusual format: rather than presenting prepared papers, participants were invited to outline some of their main ideas in order to initiate discussion. They were organised in a spirit of radical interdisciplinarity. As the transcripts of the sessions show, researchers from a wide variety of fields made substantial efforts (and struggled) to understand each other, drawing connections between diverse areas of expertise. Concepts could travel across disciplinary boundaries, sometimes taking on broader significance than initially intended, thus opening up transdisciplinary communication channels.

The Macy conferences were yet another instantiation of institutionalised serendipity, this time constructed as temporary events. Although they shouldn't be seen as the exclusive institution for the advance of the new universal science, what one encounters in them is the further formation of cybernetics as contact language and vehicle of interdisciplinary exchange of a qualitative new order.

However, the Macy conferences also marked a shift in the orientation and political context of cybernetics. While during the war, scientists were unified in the struggle against fascism, this situation obviously changed with the onset of the Cold War. For Wiener, figurehead of cybernetics during the war, the mobilisation of science in the confrontation with Russia clearly presented radically different ethical problems. According to him, contributing to the nuclear arms race that could lead to the annihilation of humankind was something that went against the ethos of scientific research. Wiener's ethical and political stance here, as summarised by Richard Barbrook, was that in "the epoch of corporate monopoly and atomic weaponry, the theory that explained the behaviour of both humans and machines must be used to place humans in control of their machines".[118] Failure to do so, Wiener warned, would open Pandora's cyberbox.

Fortunately for the sponsors of the American military-industrial-academic complex, there were others more than willing to take Wiener's place, most notably John von Neumann. Under his aegis cybernetics mutated into the study of artificial intelligence. It was founded on the idea that the processes in the human brain that lead to the emergence of consciousness are essentially calculations. Like Alan Turing before him and Ray Kurzweil later, von Neumann believed that constant progress in the development of hardware would eventually lead to the advent of sentient machines. With generous funding from the US military, von Neumann and his collaborators pushed the US onto the leading edge of computer development, with IBM becoming the dominant corporation, transferring the use of mainframes from the military to the business world.

118 Barbrook 2007: 46.

5. Serendipitous Dreams: The Intergalactic Computer Network

While IBM and five much smaller competitors began to popularise the use of business mainframes in the 1960s, another cybernetics-related Cold War race was unfolding. This time, what was at stake was the invention of the Internet. At the time, the notion of a cybernetic gap in relation to Russia had been circulating within tech-quarters of the CIA, and with the memory of the Sputnik disaster of 1957 still vivid, the US government was bent on making the invention of the Internet an American achievement. The task was assigned to the Advanced Research Projects Agency (ARPA, later DARPA) that had been set up in 1958 to make sure that the US would gain the upper hand in the cybernetic race with the Russians. In 1962, J.C.R. Licklider, a mathematician-psychologist who had participated in the Macy conferences in the Fifties, became head of ARPA's Information Processing Techniques Office (IPTO), with the primary goal of creating a unified information network. Under Licklider's leadership, ARPA generously supported Paul Baran's work on packet switching[119] at the US Air Force's research institute, the RAND Corporation, that became the foundation for ARPANET, the predecessor of today's Internet. Well before joining ARPA, Licklider had been a visionary of "cooperative interaction" by way of "man-computer symbiosis". He anticipated the emergence of the internet as a "network of [thinking centres]... connected to one another by wide-band communication lines and to individual users by leased-wire services".[120] As director of ARPA's IPTO, he was in a position to fund the work leading to the actualisation of his vision.

119 I.e., disassembling data into tiny addressed packages, sending them through high-speed lines, and reassembling them just before they reach their receiver.

120 Licklider 1960: 7.

What was at stake for Licklider was a form of cooperative creativity that was to be located at a higher lever of collaboration and intelligence. He initiated a number of computer time-sharing experiments at MIT and elsewhere, thus encouraging researchers to hard-wire, as it were, the logic of the academic gift economy into the technology of the Internet they were developing. In the 1940s, his friend Norbert Wiener had laid the foundations for the development of computing under conditions of institutionalised serendipity in the labs and hallways of MIT. Now Licklider saw an opportunity to technologically extrapolate these conditions for collective knowledge creation onto the architecture of what he referred to in a famous 1963 memo as the "intergalactic computer network". As Richard Barbrook argues, Licklider's goal with regard to computer-mediated communications was really the facilitation of scientific idiosyncrasy and collaboration by sharing knowledge.

ARPANET as the first iteration of today's Internet can thus be seen as the cybernetic materialisation of institutionalised serendipity, merging the academic gift economy with the cybernetic dream of self-organisation and self-governance through constant feedback loops. Although the invention of the Internet depended on massive military funding, it is true that the people who built it also ran it. Regardless of what has become of the Internet today, it appears to have indeed been conceived and developed as one big serendipity machine. In the context of the development of the discipline of cybernetics, ARPANET was the result of a research culture where academic collaboration had become a radically transversal affair, institutionalising the practice of interdisciplinary serendipity in a number of different ways.

Yet, while it is indeed fascinating to see that the scientific foundations of our current techno-cultural state of affairs have been laid within the paradoxical settings of cybernetic serendipity, this tells only half the story. From what we have touched upon so far, we can neither draw a straight line to the egalitarian peer-to-peer fantasies of 1990s cyberculture, nor can we understand the quasi-religious belief in the beneficial nature of digital technology that pervades our social imaginary today. In order to understand the mysterious ethical and political charge carried by digital technology and its makers we have to turn to the counterculture, and particularly to the strange symbiosis it developed with cybernetic thinking and the technological innovations of cybernetics.

6. Acid Dreams: A Different Kind of Serendipity

With the serendipitous collaborations happening at the heart of the military-industrial-academic complex safely hidden from public view, for the young generation of the Fifties and Sixties, this kind of research was regarded as part and parcel of a fatal logic of technological rationalisation that held American society in its grip. With the onset of the nuclear arms race, the logic of technological rationalisation seemed to have pushed the world to the brink of nuclear holocaust. While nuclear anxieties ran high among young Americans, so did distrust of the establishment and its bureaucratic organisation. The Vietnam War reinforced the sentiment of society being at the mercy of a technological bureaucracy whose centralised apparatus was, quite literally, out of control. At the time, authors such as C. Wright Mills and Lewis Mumford struck a nerve with their young contemporaries by pointing toward a dystopian future in which automation destroyed American values such as individuality and freedom of expression.[121] The convergence of technological progress and bureaucratic structure, they argued, had produced a Behemoth that would turn American society into a well-functioning system of docile automata. While William Whyte's *The Organization Man*

121   Mills 2000 [1959]; Mumford 1967.

epitomised the uncreative boredom of corporate conformity, Mills' "cheerful robot" was the truly frightening *telos* of hierarchised hyper-rationality.[122]

As a reaction to these developments, two related yet rather diverging social movements arose throughout the US. On the one hand, the New Left emerged, with its roots in the civil rights struggles of the American South as well as the Free Speech Movement. This movement was emphatically political, playing a leading role in the protests against the Vietnam War. Their strategy was to confront the establishment through activism, the founding of new parties, or, indeed, political protest. What was 'new' about the New Left was their shift from classical Marxist positions that prioritised class struggle towards more cultural issues such as gender, racism, abortion, etc. On the other hand, there was the counterculture and hippie movement that grew out of subcultures like the Beatniks, who were influenced by Eastern philosophy and expressive art forms and, of course, had an intimate relationship with drugs, such as Marijuana, but above all LSD. What differentiated the countercultural hippies from their colleagues in the New Left was their strategy of exodus. While the New Left tried to carry its issues into the system, the counterculture tried to escape 'back to the land'. They had lost their confidence in the institution of politics *per se* and were trying to create new ways of living emphatically 'outside' the structures of society.

It is indeed the latter of these two movements that came to form an intriguingly intimate relationship with the rhetoric (and innovations) of cybernetics later on. Yet, before we turn to this fateful encounter, let us first take a brief look at the counterculture itself. Again, what interests me here is the culture

122 For an interesting contemporary survey of the countercultural landscape of the 1960s see O'Neill 1971, Chapter 8.

of serendipity that in the case of the counterculture was much less institutionalised than its counterpart in secret cybernetics research labs. The epicentre of the American counterculture was San Francisco's Haight-Ashbury district that since the early Sixties had developed into a vibrant neo-Bohemia, attracting misfits of all stripes. As Martin A. Lee and Bruce Shlain describe in great detail in their wonderful *Acid Dreams*, it was above all under the influence of LSD that the Haight became the nexus of a form of social experimentation that favoured the expansion of the mind over political struggle. From the Acid-Test parties, to the Be-ins and the massive Summer of Love – with lots of things happening in between – an orgy of unexpected encounters unfolded that saw bikers mingling with Buddhists, radicals with pacifists, rock musicians with poets, and so on and so forth. While this didn't necessarily produce processes that would correspond to Merton's definition of serendipity in a strict sense, it did generate an atmosphere in which a much funkier kind of accidental sagacity was likely to happen at high frequency. From San Francisco, a great wave of cultural and social innovation began to wash over the United States. It revolutionised popular music, fashion, religion and also, perhaps most importantly, set off an entire plethora of experiments in social organisation. Augustus Owsley Stanley III, legendary acid manufacturer and unofficial 'mayor of San Francisco' put it:

> We believed that we were the architects of social change, that our mission was to change the world substantially, and what was going on in the Haight was a sort of laboratory experiment, a microscopic sample of what would happen worldwide.[123]

123 Lee & Shlain 1985: 147.

Apart from the hedonism of sex and drugs and psychedelic rock & roll, there was indeed a countercultural vision that led the search for different forms of thinking and doing, of a different kind of community outside society. Change in society, as Timothy Leary articulated the hippie-ethos, was to be brought about not by politics or rebellion but by religion. The social change that began with the change (or substance-assisted expansion) of mind required no strategy or democratic process, it was a question of setting the spiritual power free through all sorts of cultural and social experiments, and evangelising the rest of society and the planet. And from the point of view of tens of thousands of youth flocking to that San Francisco neighbourhood, it might indeed have seemed to work like that.

Today, of course, we are quite aware as to the romantic hubris this vision was based on.[124] And yet it was quite a trip, and an enormous exercise in social innovation. One of the interesting things here is that social 'change' functioned rather differently from what the gurus had in mind. Not unlike today's bureaucrats of 'social innovation', they believed that the 'thought leaders' could somehow control the prototypes they developed and scale them onto global society. What happened, of course, was that the prototypes developed in the 'authentic' space-time of countercultural experiments entered the social process in order to be changed, inverted, perverted, refined and so on. Society, one might say, did what it always does, i.e., changing the change. Yet, while the orgy of countercultural serendipity might not have made 'the world a better place' in the way intended by its leaders, the temporary exodus from the social norms and conventions of the time paved the way for many of the cultural innovations that

---

124   The historical parallels to the (very) late Romantic movements of the early 20th century, particular in Germany, are indeed striking. See, e.g., Safranski 2009, Chapters 15 and 16.

are still with us today. As always, it was from the fringes of society that mainstream culture had some of its previously closed doors kicked in, through which innovation could then travel.

The perhaps most interesting development with respect to the present inquiry was the dispersion of experiments in social organisation from San Francisco to other American cities, as well as the hinterland. These "New Communialists", as Fred Turner has baptised them, tended to organise themselves around religious, sexual, or political beliefs. The movement of the New Communalists reached its apex in the early Seventies, when their number, according to some estimates, reached somewhere around 750,000 throughout the US. While the communities were indeed spread throughout the US, their highest concentration and visibility was in California and on the East Coast. It is within the New Communalists that the fateful encounter between mind-expanding hippies and cybernetics begins as a public affair.[125]

7. Branding the Encounter: Love meets War

The crucial figure in this encounter was Stewart Brand. Brand was very much a child of his time, both in terms of his distrust in politics and his aversion to hierarchical organisation. Like many of his generation, he was looking for new approaches to personal and collective liberation upon which a way out of the deadlock of post-war culture and politics could be developed. While a student at Stanford, he had become acquainted with cybernetic thinking through Paul Ehrlich's system-oriented approaches to evolutionary biology. What fascinated Brand with regard to cybernetics

125 Which is not to say that there was no contact between those worlds before. There was, mainly at the universities. Most of the hippie gurus were intellectuals and aware of the developments in the field of cybernetics. Some of them, like Stewart Brand or Ken Kesey, were actually hippies, while others, like Buckminster Fuller, converted over from the military-academic complex.

and systems thinking was that it offered a new and seemingly productive way to understanding social power relations. If the cybernetic reduction could be applied to the social world as well, this seemed to imply that the human factor was only one among many – ranging from spiritual to technological – and thus pointed at least conceptually to the possibility of taking part in a process of social innovation that did not have to rely on the ossified institutions of traditional politics.

In the early Sixties, Brand began to travel between New York and San Francisco, working with countercultural collectives and communes on both coasts. In San Francisco, Brand met the novelist Ken Kesey (author of *One Flew Over the Cuckoo's Nest*) and joined his commune, the Merry Pranksters.[126] The Pranksters epitomised the Californian brand of psychedelic counterculture, who, in spite of their rejection of the technological-bureaucratic apparatus of Cold War America, embraced the media technologies it produced. Rather than rejecting technology *per se*, they tried to appropriate it for their consciousness expanding practices (including, of course, the pharmaceutical technology called LSD).[127] During their famous cross-country tour of 1964, their bus

126 The classical account on the Merry Pranksters, that was simultaneously an exercise in the then so-called New Journalism, remains Wolfe 1968.

127 It might be worth mentioning that the discovery of LSD had also been a product of serendipity. In 1938, Swiss chemist Albert Hofmann synthesised LSD (lysergic acid diethylamide) for the first time at Sandoz Labs in Switzerland as part of an analysis of ergot, a rye fungus with high contents of medicinal alkaloids. He was searching for an analeptic compound, i.e., a circulatory stimulant. Preliminary tests didn't show a significant effect and so the drug was shelved until one faithful afternoon in April 1943. Years later, Hofmann described his serendipitous encounter with the drug as follows: "I had a strange feeling... that it would be worthwhile to carry out more profound studies with this compound." In the course of preparing a fresh batch of LSD he accidentally absorbed a small dose through his fingertips, and soon he was overcome by "a remarkable but not unpleasant state of intoxication ... characterized by an intense stimulation of the imagination and an altered state of

was stacked with audio gadgetry to capture random sounds along the road as well as enable communication inside the bus.[128]

Similar sound installations were to be found as Kesey's home in rural La Honda, creating a backdrop of sound environments for drug-enhanced accidental encounters between nature, technology and humans that would make the hearts of contemporary actor-network theorists leap for joy.[129] The public events, such as Kesey's Acid Tests, created even richer high-tech environments for the sake of consciousness expansion. As Mark Dery summarises the techno-serendipitous ethos of the Californian rebels:

> The inhabitants of the sixties counterculture exemplified by Kesey and his Pranksters may have dreamed of enlightenment, but theirs was the 'plug-and-play' nirvana of the 'gadget-happy American' – cosmic consciousness on demand, attained not through long years of Siddhartha-like questing but instantaneously, by chemical means, amidst the sensory assault of a high-tech happening.[130]

When not tripping with the Merry Pranksters in California, Brand mingled with the more intellectualist East Coast art scene.

awareness of the world. ... As I lay in a dazed condition with eyes closed there surged up from me a succession of fantastic, rapidly changing imagery of a striking reality and depth, alternating with a vivid, kaleidoscopic play of colors. This condition gradually passed off after about three hours." (quoted in Lee & Shlain 1985: XVIII).

128 "A Prankster could listen to the various sound sources simultaneously, on headphones, and free-associate into a microphone hooked up to a tape delay system, improvising over layers of his own echoed words." (Dery 1996: 29).

129 As the generous Brian Holmes reminded me, William Burroughs was the European forerunner of these practices in his collaborations with the avant-garde poetry circles of the time. They were all adept with the recorder; they would improvise, cut and remix the tapes, etc. See Burroughs 1970.

130 Dery 1996: 29.

In New York, he was affiliated with the art collective USCO (US Company) that at the time was at the cutting edge of an art scene busy exploring new ways of artistic expression, emphasising the collaborative nature of the artist's process in relation to both their materials and audiences. Emblematic of these kinds of explorations were John Cage's experiments with the aleatory, or chance, in music (extended into the world of modern dance by his collaborator and partner Merce Cunningham), the action painting of Robert Rauschenberg, or the 'happenings' by performance artist Allan Kaprow. What these and other avant-garde artists articulated in their practice was an attempt to depart from the 'human-centric' notion of the artist as creative hero, instead trying to flatten creative authorship onto artistic systems wherein materials, audiences and artists collaborated as equals. Such an anti-hierarchical attitude was often supported by a strong influence of Eastern, psychedelic and 'back to nature' philosophies. Yet, although these collaborative systems of colliding energy currents and spiritual oneness were of quite a different order than the techno-scientific collaborations of the military research labs, in some respects they were not miles away from cybernetic serendipity. Their more mystical approach to technology was on par with cybernetics when it came to facilitating multidisciplinary collaboration. USCO's productions, for instance, ranged from psychedelic posters and three-dimensional poems to multimedia shows. Each production, as Turner points out, required input by artists with a variety of technical skills, and the collaboration in turn required both a contact language in which the artists could speak to one another and a rationale to drive their production. Techno-mysticism fitted both bills. "Like the anti-aircraft gunner operating Wiener's theoretical predictor," he writes, "they could see themselves as parts of a techno-social system, serving new machines and being served by them." [131]

Not quite halfway but somewhere in between the scholarly efforts of the cyberneticists and the lifestyle experimentations of the Californian hippies, the avant-garde artists with whom Brand mingled were looking for a way out of the post-war cultural deadlock by merging new media enthusiasm and New Age philosophy. Out of this they created a serendipitous practice whereby techno-mysticism functioned as a platform for communication, enabling interdisciplinary encounters for the sake of artistic innovation. Techno-mysticism, one might say, served as an anti-institutional form of institutionalised serendipity.

In the above quote, Turner likens the collaborative effect of techno-mysticism to the serendipitous interface (contact language) the interdisciplinarity of cybernetics provided. While the ontological reduction Wiener and his colleagues performed turned the human being into an info-mechanical element of a cybernetic system, the artistic explorers of USCO tried to liberate the human being from the coercive institutions of post-war America by a rather similar operation. By flattening the ontology of the artist onto a system in which new technologies and mythological forces worked on equal footings for the achievement of a systemic goal, they could invoke the powers of technology and myth as means of countercultural fortification.

In spite of their different roots – avant-garde art on the East Coast and Beatniks on the West Coast – the two countercultures had of course quite a bit of common ground. Disillusioned with the institutions of the American establishment, they both rejected the classical modern process of politics in favour of a technology-immersed experimental exodus into a participative, communal future. The occasion that perhaps best articulated the

---

131 Turner 2006: 58.

conversion of the two countercultures was the Trips Festival that took place in early 1966 in Haight-Ashbury. Effectively, this was a fusion of Kesey's earlier Acid Tests and USCO-like multimedia happenings. According to Lee and Shlain, the Trips Festival

> was a wide-open three-day LSD party with just about every sight and sound imaginable: mime exhibitions, guerrilla theatre, a 'Congress of Wonders', and live mikes and sound equipment for everyone to play with. Closed-circuit television cameras were set up on the dance floor so people could watch themselves shake and swing. Music blasted at ear splitting volumes while Day-Glo bodies bounced gleefully on trampolines. At one point Kesey flashed from a projector, 'Anyone who knows he is God please go up on stage'.[132]

The Trips festival created an environment of sensuous overflow, a laboratory where countercultural energies and currents could be creatively de- and reassembled. It curated a human-media(machine)-drug interface upon which the spiritual communion of an alter-America could be celebrated. By doing so, it provided a prototype of a countercultural innovation machine that ran on the liberating ecstasy of a techno-mysticism able to send the young generation off to a new and much more open world. The Trips Festival, which also served as the kick-off to the popularisation (and commercialisation) of the Haight-Ashbury phenomenon across the US, was the countercultural equivalent of the Macy conferences: a radically inter-'disciplinary' openness merged with a techno-mystical contact-ideology in order to give birth to a strangely institutionalised alter-serendipity that turned the Sixties into the countercultural innovation feast whose reverberation we feel until this day.

132   Lee & Shlain 1985: 143.

8. Common Ground: The *Whole Earth Catalogue*

There were two thinkers who helped shape this important blend of techno-euphoria and mysticism: Marshall McLuhan and Buckminster Fuller. While both of them were fervently anti-political thinkers of technology, McLuhan articulated the techno-mysticism of the Sixties in terms of a theory of social evolution characterised by a radical technological determinism, whereas Fuller introduced a comprehensive notion of design as a techno-humanist alternative to politics. For Stewart Brand, Buckminster Fuller's comprehensive designer became something of a blueprint for his own professional development. Brand, who already had some experience as a designer of temporary ecologies of seren-dipitous creativity from the USCO happenings and the Trips Fes-tival, turned himself into the personification of a comprehensive designer with the creation of the *Whole Earth Catalogue*. Founded by Brand in 1968, the *Whole Earth Catalogue* began its existence as a six-page mimeographed salesman's catalogue with which Brand travelled to the different communes that were popping up in the south of the US. It contained offers on a variety of technical gear, camping supplies, construction plans for alternative buildings and machines, but also relevant books or magazine subscriptions. Over the next few years, Brand turned these few initial sheets into a 448-sheet book that in 1971 even received the National Book Award.

At that point, it had mutated from a traditional travelling salesman's catalogue containing supplies for communal living to a dynamically growing medium curated by Brand yet sustained by the community of its readers. For although it was impossi-ble to directly mail-order the great variety of items listed in the catalogue, what readers could do is to write to Brand in order to contribute reviews, comment on other readers' reviews, or sug-gest new items to be included in future issues of the catalogue.

It is in this sense that Steve Jobs was almost spot on when referring to the *Whole Earth Catalogue* as being "sort of like Google
in paperback form, 35 years before Google came along".[133] Where
the analogy holds is in the catalogue's role as a pre-Internet communication platform, a sort of printed chat room still restrained
by the limitations of the Gutenberg Galaxy but already pointing
beyond it. This somewhat strange yet highly innovative piece of
communication technology articulated for the first time the con-
fluence of cybernetics and counterculture. Networking "the world
of university-, government- and industry-based science and technology; the New York and San Francisco art scenes; the Bay area
psychedelic community; and the communes that sprang up across
America in the late 1960s",[134] the *Whole Earth Catalogue* served as
a medium and icon for what in today's innovation lingua would be
called 'intellectual synergies' and 'cross-pollination':

> When these groups met in its pages, the *Catalogue* became the
> single most visible publication in which the technological and
> intellectual output of industry and high science met the Eastern
> religion, acid mysticism, and communal social theory of the
> back-to-the-land movement. It also became the home and emblem
> of a new, geographically distributed community. As they flipped
> through and wrote in to its several editions, contributors and
> readers peered across the social and intellectual fences of their
> home communities. Like the collaborative researchers of World
> War II, they became interdisciplinarians, cobbling together new
> understandings of the ways in which information and technology
> might reshape social life.[135]

133 Jobs made this remark at his 2005 commencement address at Stanford
University.
134 Turner 2006: 73.
135 Ibid.

The *Whole Earth Catalogue* represented a highly innovative communication tool emphatically directed toward the needs and purposes of the New Communalists, but in fact it reached far beyond them. As it bridged the cybernetic and countercultural scenes and communities, combining their attitudes and expertise, it reflected an emerging cultural orientation that evolved into the belief-system of the 'digital revolution'. Many of the decisive elements can be found in the *Catalogue*: small-scale technology, consciousness development, entrepreneurialism, heterarchical organisation, virtual community and, of course, a general techno-mysticism.

While the *Whole Earth Catalogue* was the bible of the counterculture in California and elsewhere, it also helped to spread the cultural symbiosis of cybernetics and rebellion beyond the community of rebels proper. It codified the radical gospel, thus making it available as a cultural meme, an expression of the zeitgeist, a symbol of rebellious attitude. In this sense, the catalogue helped to preserve the ethos of counterculture while simultaneously detaching it from the immediate practice that had originally spawned it.[136] And Brand did it just in time, as for the countercultural communities the Seventies were a decade of steady decline. Their practical attempt at an exodus from society proved unsustainable in the medium run. The countercultural brew of consciousness expansion, small scale techno-fetishism and mystical tribalism turned out to be a great source of inspiration, but was no match for the real internal and external pressures the communards had to face up to eventually.

---

136 For an interesting reassessment of the *Whole Earth Catalogue* in the context of the 'Anthropocene' art project at the Haus der Kulturen der Welt in Berlin see Franke & Diedrichsen 2013.

9. Climbing out of the Valley: Innovation's Sagacity

The collapse of the countercultural rebellion in the 1970s coincided with the beginning of a geographically concentrated cascade of technological innovations that the journalist Don Hoefler in 1971 marked with the term "Silicon Valley". What I wanted to show in this chapter is that the emergence of the 'digital revolution' out of the Santa Clara Valley (and later the southern San Francisco Bay area) was to a large extent determined by social processes whose motivation and direction had absolutely nothing to do with creating a start-up hub for the digital industry. These were two distinct movements of social innovation, one unfolding in the context of military conflict, the other as an attempt to exit a world shaped by such a conflict. While the serendipitous culture of cybernetics flourished in the shadow of the military apparatus where the logic of scientific exploration was at least partly protected from the searchlights of market and immediate valorisation, the counterculture managed, at least temporarily, to create a refuge for their serendipitous escapades in the shadow of the land.[137]

We have seen above that with regard to the scholarly side of the story, a surprisingly open research culture emerged within the secretive belly of the military-industrial-academic beast.

137 To speak, as I have done throughout this chapter, of 'cultures of serendipity' is in no way meant as an attempt to reduce either one of those trajectories to their serendipitous character. It would be silly to claim that serendipity exhaustively defined either the research labs or the hippie culture. Yet, it was the crucial ingredient that in both cases spawned practices that were highly creative and inventive. They both were driven by the intuitive and sometimes explicit realisation that systematically crossing disciplinary and/ or normative borders is a promising path for those who engage in the paradox of looking for novelty. And for rather specific historical reasons, the academics as well as the countercultural youth were able to create environments and practices that pushed the logic of serendipitous exploration into previously uncharted territory.

Conditioned first by the unified ambition to defeat fascism and later by the goal to win the Cold War, this led to the creation of the new and radical interdisciplinary project of cybernetics that in fact instantiated Robert Merton's idea of institutionalised serendipity. By virtue of increasingly functioning as a contact language among a wide variety of academic disciplines, cybernetics even accelerated the logic of serendipitous interdisciplinarity. It is certainly true that the context within which scientific serendipity was institutionalised determined to a substantial degree the output of cybernetic research. The paradox is that while relying on informal and idiosyncratic forms of interpersonal exchange, cybernetics spawned a techno-social ontology, reducing human beings to increasingly calculable, controllable and predictable factors within systems. It invented a practice of serendipity but simultaneously infected our thinking about ourselves and the world with what Peter Galison famously called "the ontology of the enemy" that has become the greatest inhibitor of the actual occurrence of accidental sagacity.[138]

Yet, before the cybernetic trajectory could be pushed down this road, its encounter with the other culture of serendipity, the hippie movement, laid the foundation for the 'digital revolution'. Ostensibly as a rejection of a society shaped by the logic of techno-scientific progress, countercultural forms of artistic, social and lifestyle experimentation emerged in the Sixties that were every bit as serendipitous as their scientific counterpart. Obviously, the countercultural exodus into the Californian hippie utopia and the New Communalists would hardly qualify as forms of institu-

138 We see this clearly expressed in the dystopian visions of so-called Smart Cities and the Internet of Things, where the population is strictly conceived as an enemy to be kept in check by means of total digital control, down to the strategies of self-quantification where the self is pitted against itself in a personal war against unhappiness, inefficiency and all kinds of perceived illnesses.

tionalised serendipity in Merton's sense. Instead, the innovative power of countercultural serendipity emerged from a generation of disillusioned youngsters who took refuge in a parallel universe that for a time seemed to be unencumbered by many of the conventions and 'squareness' of mainstream institutions. Like it or not, we would not have the digital culture and economy we have today if it wasn't for the counterculture of the Sixties. It was the hippies who engaged in the collective – or rather, communal – search for a radically different society that fed into the early business culture of Silicon Valley. The wave of technological and indeed cultural change initiated by the likes of Steve Jobs was inspired by the search for radically different social practices. I obviously don't mean this as a further glorification of the digital demigod. My point is that substantial innovation, i.e., innovation that really has a sustained impact on wider society, is not something that comes about by trying to recreate already existing conditions of previous innovations.

The real lesson that can be drawn from Silicon Valley in terms of the social conditions necessary for future innovation is thus quite simple: on the one hand, well funded academic infrastructures unencumbered by the logic of market and valorisation; on the other hand, a strong commitment to a politics of public space that leaves enough room for the non-utilitarian explorations of subcultures, artists and all sorts of misfits in the margins of society. While this would not, of course, guarantee anything, it would at least create the social conditions under which new waves of serendipitous practices *could* be triggered. Paradoxically, one of the great hindrances of the creation of these basic conditions for future innovation is a belief system brought about by the encounter of cybernetics and counterculture as well. Throughout the Eighties and even more so during the Nineties, the countercultural vision of a better world was transformed into a worldview that has found its imperfect yet apposite expression in Richard

Barbrook and Andy Cameron's notion of the *Californian Ideology*: a vacuous marketing religion for the digital industry. As such, it became the ideological veneer that helped to veil the neoliberal degeneration of our economies and societies whose consequences have been vividly described by the likes of Naomi Klein, Thomas Piketty and many others. Today, any meaningful attempt at innovation, in so far as it is understood as an effort to reshape society for the sake of a sustainable future, would necessarily have to entail a departure from both.

VI Never Mind the Sharing Economy:
Here's Platform Capitalism

1. The Hype Is Over! Or Is It?

After years of unequivocal enthusiasm over its innovative wonders, the public seems to be waking up to the ambivalences of
the 'sharing economy'. Although the social media blogosphere
and marketing channels continue to churn out the sharing credo,
the celebratory tone is increasingly countered by articles warning
their readers not to buy into the sharing hype, or denouncing it
as a straight-out lie.[139] Mainstream media is joining in as well. In
May 2014, the American business magazine *Forbes* got wary about
a "backlash against the sharing economy".[140] Yet, while *Forbes*
seemed convinced that the sharing economy is here to stay, its
ideological brother in arms, *Fast Company*, declared a year later
that "The Sharing Economy is Dead".[141] Meanwhile, across the
pond, the new mayor of Barcelona, Ado Colau, didn't give a damn
about the boom and bust of hype cycles, and simply declared war
on the sharing economy, or at least on one of its poster boys, by
banning AirBnB. Likewise, in Spring 2015, UberPop was banned in
the whole of Germany. Other European countries and cities were
to follow the German example.

For Trebor Scholz, associate professor at New York's New
School for Social Research and an expert on sharing models,
developments like these show that, ideologically speaking, the

139 E.g., Eskow 2015, Scheiber 2014.
140 Kaufman 2014.
141 Kessler 2015.

sharing economy is more or less over. He writes at the online publishing platform medium.com:

> [B]y now, only few people still fall for the solidarity theater of
> the 'disruptive sharing economy', its deceptive 'peer' rhetoric
> when referring to individual workers and consumers, as well as
> its constant talk of changing the world... They figured it out by
> now. People understand that it is the *modus operandi* of the
> 'community managers' of the sharing economy to conflate
> multimillion-dollar commercial entities like *Uber* with non-
> market, peer-to-peer projects like *Wikipedia* or *FoldIt*.

While one would hope for Scholz to be right, I am afraid his assessment as to the ineffectiveness of sharing rhetoric is altogether pre-
mature. For those of us professionally concerned with the matter,
it may seem fairly easy to deflate the pompous spiel of community
managers and sharing marketeers. However, neither does this
mean that the news has got through to the majority of the public
or, for that matter, to the majority of our municipal, national and
transnational policy makers. In fact, the latter continue to give the
impression that they can hardly contain their enthusiasm (unless
they are either radical leftist Catalonians or Germans).[142] And so

142 In December 2013, the United States Conference of Mayors passed a
resolution, vowing to encourage the growth of the sharing economy in their
cities (The United States Conference of Mayors 2013). In November 2014, the
British government published a report announcing its intention to turn the
UK into a global centre for the sharing economy before 2020 (Wosskow 2014,
also Arthur 2014). As Business and Enterprise Minister Matthew Hancock
rejoiced: "The sharing economy is an exciting new area of the economy. Digital
innovation is creating entirely new ways to do business. These new services are
unlocking a new generation of microentrepreneurs – people who are making
money from the assets and skills they already own, from renting out a spare
room through Airbnb, through to working as a freelance designer through
PeoplePerHour. The route to self-employment has never been easier."
(Wosskow 2014: 6.)

does PricewaterhouseCoopers, who predict that global revenue for the sharing economy could rise from $15 billion today to $335 billion in 2025.

Thus, there is reason enough to engage once more in the debate around sharing. This is what this chapter sets out to do. Whatever the sharing economy really stands for, it appears to be a force to be reckoned with; not just in quantitative terms but also in terms of the infrastructural transformations it pushes for. The proponents of the sharing economy, this much is clear, want to change the face of capitalism on the back of what they believe to be a seren-dipitous convergence of digital and mobile technology, economic crisis and cultural reorientation.[143] What this chapter wants to find out is to whose benefit the infrastructural disruptions of the sharing economy work. Should we embrace – perhaps at least parts of – the sharing economy as a force for good that helps to create a fairer, more participatory economy? Or are there good reasons for the mobilisation of sagacious resistance against it?

2. To Share or Not to Share

Not unlike other contemporary policy fashions and economic megatrends, the sharing economy throws together a variety of diverse and often unrelated phenomena; from massively funded technology start-ups like Uber or AirBnB to fair trade coopera-tives, borrowing shops and hippie communes. It would be wrong, however, to understand this confusion as a result of the intel-lectual incompetence on the side of trend watchers and innova-tion consultants. While it is true that the growing army of these professional would-be clairvoyants depends on the regular con-struction of the 'next big thing' for their own economic survival

---

143 *The Economist* (2014), for instance, is convinced that "[t]he sharing economy is one of the great unforeseen benefits of the digital age."

– the more confused the better for the business – the notion of the sharing economy is much less a conceptual confusion than it is a smart marketing strategy.

The first thing we need to understand about the sharing economy is that it has absolutely nothing to do with sharing in the sense you and I might think about it. The essence of sharing – if it has any meaning at all – is of course that it does not involve the exchange of money. Sharing only happens in the absence of market transactions. With regard to the poster boys and girls of the sharing movement, the very opposite is the case. These are digital platforms that roughly do two things: either making the old practice of re- and multi-using durable goods more efficient, or expanding market exchange into an economically uncharted territory of society.

If we look at Internet marketplaces such as Ebay, Etsy and their many variations, it is clear that what they offer are digitally modernised versions of the good old second hand shop. What's new about them is that thanks to the Internet, the supply of used goods (and in the case of Etsy, also handicraft) finds its demand much more efficiently than ever before. There can be no doubt that this leads to a more efficient (re-)use of durable goods, thus contributing to a more sustainable allocation of resources. The same applies to rentals, particular with regard to cars or bikes but also lots of other goods. Thanks to the Internet and mobile digital technology, the centralised stockpiling of goods to be rented has become unnecessary, which, again, saves resources. Their dispersion is not a problem anymore but often rather adds to the convenience of the rental – think of a car that you can pick up around the corner rather than having to travel to the nearest agent. However, none of this has anything to do with sharing! Matthew Yglesias, writing for the US online magazine *Slate*, illustrates this fact as follows:

My neighbor and I share a snow shovel because we share some stairs that need to be shoveled when it snows and we share responsibility for doing the work. If I owned the stairs and charged him a small fee every time he walked in or out of the house, that would be the opposite of sharing.

This might sound trivial, but given the confused usage of the notion of sharing, it seems appropriate to remind ourselves that helping each other out by sharing our resources is one thing, while commodifying these resources by charging a fee for their use is quite another. Which gets us to the more innovative dimension of the sharing economy. Today, the sharing economy entails much more than just digital updates of second-hand exchange and rentals. What companies like Uber, AirBnB, TaskRabbit or Postmates have in common is that they are platforms coordinating supply and demand of products and services that in their present form were previously unavailable on the market. Uber is a platform where people looking for a cab quickly find their non-, semi-, or real professional taxi driver. AirBnB allows people to sublet their houses, TaskRabbit connects supply and demand for chores, Postmates for deliveries, Instacart for grocery shopping, and so on. While it might be convenient to make use of these services, they have absolutely nothing to do with sharing. They stand for a digitally enabled expansion of the market economy, which, again, is the opposite of sharing. If someone does my shopping or drops me at the airport in exchange for a financial fee, how is this sharing? This situation doesn't change if instead of money, one receives credits to be used at the issuing platform (a mistake that for the last few years has led to a rather annoying hype in 'alternative currencies' based on the belief that the 'evils' of capitalism could be cured by replacing real money with a less efficient substitute).

3. Enter Platform Capitalism

To overcome this confusion, I would suggest dropping the obscure notion of the sharing economy altogether. Here, I agree with Sascha Lobo, a German technology blogger for *Der Spiegel*, who argues that "what is called the sharing economy is merely one aspect of a more general development, i.e., a new quality of the digital economy: platform capitalism". As Lobo emphasises, platforms like Uber and AirBnB are more than just Internet marketplaces. While marketplaces connect supply and demand between customers and companies, digital platforms connect customers to whatever. Platforms in this sense are indeed generic 'ecosystems' able to link potential customers to anything and anyone, from private individuals to multinational corporations. Everyone can become a supplier for all sorts of products and services at the click of a button. This is the real innovation that companies of the platform capitalist variety have introduced. It doesn't necessarily need to turn us into "perpetual hustlers", as internet critic Evgeny Morozov writes in *the Guardian*, but it is definitely miles away from sharing. It represents a mutation of our economic system enabled by the application of digital technology.

Switching from 'sharing economy' to 'platform capitalism' is by no means a matter of linguistic nit-picking. Calling this crucial development by its proper name is an important step towards a more sober assessment of the claims made by the proponents of sharing. Take, for instance, the notion that everyone benefits from the disruptive force of the sharing economy because it cuts out the middleman. Sharing models, the argument goes, facilitate a more direct exchange between economic agents, thus eliminating the inefficient middle layers and making market exchange simpler and fairer. While it is absolutely true that Internet marketplaces and digital platforms can reduce transaction costs, the claim that they cut out the middleman is pure fantasy. Indeed, old middlemen and retailers disappear, but only to be replaced by much more powerful gatekeepers.

In fact, the argument of the disappearing middleman is quite an obscene one, particularly if it is made by the stakeholders of platform capitalism themselves. As globally operating digital platforms, these companies have the unique ability to cut across many regional markets and reconfigure traditionally specific markets for goods and services as generic customer-to-whatever 'ecosystems'. "The uncomfortable truth", Izabella Kaminska writes in the *Financial Times*, "is that the sharing economy is a rent-extraction business of the highest middleman order." It seems fairly obvious that the entire purpose of the platform business model is to reach a monopoly position, as this enables the respective platform to set and control the (considerably lower) standards upon which someone (preferably anyone) could become a supplier in the respective market. Instead of cutting out the middleman, digital platforms have the inherent tendency to create veritable *Über-middlemen*, i.e., monopolies with an unprecedented control over the markets they themselves create. Economists denounce such strategies of extreme profiteering without value creation as "rent-seeking". Peter Thiel, outspoken mouthpiece of successful tech-investment, has recently summarised the entrepreneurial ethos of Silicon Valley in the motto "competition is for losers", and it seems that the new platforms capitalists have taken more than a page from his book. In fact, even technically speaking, calling these customer-to-whatever ecosystems 'markets' often turns out to be a bit of a joke. For Uber & co, price is not the result of the free play of supply and demand, but of specific algorithms supposedly simulating the market mechanism. The effect of such algorithmic market simulation is demonstrated for instance by Uber's surge pricing during periods of peak demand. It is not very difficult to see where this might be leading. Taking a cab to the hospital in New York City during a snow storm might become unaffordable for some under conditions of mature platform capitalism, as might be getting away from a hostage situation in, say, Sydney's city centre.

4. Getting into the Sharing Economy

Taxi drivers and their clients are of course not the only ones who are affected by the spread of platform capitalism. The point of the customer-to-whatever model entails that everyone can be a supplier or vendor selling their products and services on a growing variety of platforms. Part of the appeal of platform-induced sharing is that it tails beautifully with the general cultural tendency toward more flexible and fluid lifestyles.[144] In addition, it promises a more sustainable lifestyle (resource sharing!) as well. In the words of the otherwise rather dismissive Morozov writing in *the Guardian*, this potent mixture turns the sharing economy into something like a practical fountain of youth:

> Not only does it help to deal with overconsumption – we can all get by with less if we only find a way to use existing resources more efficiently! – but it also gives those on the receiving end of the 'sharing economy' an exhilarating sense of permanent youth. We can finally break, once and for all, with the usual traps of the boring middle-class existence: no need to settle down, own a house, buy a car, fill the basement with clunky household appliances. It's all there, in the cloud, to be rented and delivered by drones.

However, the success of platform capitalism is not just down to lifestyle. It is no coincidence that platform capitalism emerges at a moment of global financial and economic crisis. In the absence

144 Zygmunt Bauman marks this tendency with the notion of "liquid modernity" whose different aspects he analyses in quite a number of publications (e.g., Bauman 2000, 2003, 2006).

of employment opportunities and the invention of zero hour contracts, sharing platforms provide an attractive alternative with a very low entry threshold. If we are to believe the proponents of the sharing economy, then the opportunities are pretty amazing. As Brian Chesky, CEO and cofounder of Airbnb, puts it in an interview with Wall Street Journal's Andy Kessler:

> I want to live in a world where people can become entrepreneurs or micro-entrepreneurs and if we can lower the friction and inspire them to do that, especially in an economy like today, this is the promise of the sharing economy.

According to Chesky, digital platforms like his are the way forward, as they allow people to reach their entrepreneurial aspirations even in times of dire economic prospects. *New York Magazine*'s Kevin Roose sees the sharing economy as an answer to our current economic predicament as well, but is somewhat less euphoric as to the potency of the sharing antidote:

> Tools that help people trust in the kindness of strangers might be the thing pushing hesitant sharing-economy participants over the threshold to adoption. But what's getting them to the threshold in the first place is a damaged economy, and harmful public policy that has forced millions of people to look to odd jobs for sustenance.

So which one is it then: inspired micro-entrepreneurs or "odd jobs for sustenance"? Business magazine *Fast Company*, a publication known for its enthusiasm for everything innovative and digital, has tried to find an answer to this question by sending one of its writers for one month to test the waters of entrepreneurial inspiration in the sharing economy. The conclusion of her very interesting and extensive report is rather devastating:

For one month, I became the 'micro-entrepreneur' touted by companies like *TaskRabbit*, *Postmates*, and *Airbnb*. Instead of the labor revolution I had been promised, all I found was hard work, low pay, and a system that puts workers at a disadvantage.

In fact, Sarah Kessler (that's the name of the writer turned sharing guinea pig) never made enough to get by at all despite being young, flexible and urban, i.e., part of the social cohort that is supposed to fare particularly well in the sharing economy. Similar concerns have been raised by other reports and the slowly emerging academic research into the phenomenon.[145] The picture is at least ambivalent: for those who actually *own* something *worth* sharing, platform capitalism offers a way to monetise their assets by departing from them or, indeed, making them available for others to share. For those who own no more than their labour power, things look a bit more sketchy. "[I]f you don't own anything in this ecosystem", Francisco Dao writes for *Pando*, "wrapping it up in the pretty package of the sharing economy doesn't change the fact that you are just a short term borrower of someone else's property." And if you would like to hang on to the credo of micro-entrepreneurship, then things get even more difficult. This is at least what the *New York Times* journalist Natasha Singer found in her rather comprehensive analysis of the phenomenon. Yes, there is freedom to be found in platform capitalism, but it is the precarious freedom of what the newspaper calls the "gig economy":

> Many gigs may seem to offer decent pay. But they may not look that great after factoring in the time spent, expenses, insurance costs and taxes on self-employment earnings.

145   See the studies by Schor 2015 and also Slee 2015.

In the same article, Dean Baker, economist and co-director of the Center for Economic and Policy Research in Washington, agrees: "If you did the calculations, many of these people would be earning less than minimum wage." According to his assessment, there is innovation and disruption in platform capitalism, but not in the sense many of its proponents would like us to believe. The pretence of sharing, he says, is a great way of "getting people to self-exploit in ways we have regulations in place to prevent".

5. Micro-Entrepreneurs and Platform Proletarians

It is indeed from the perspective of labour and the conditions of value creation in general that things get really interesting with platform capitalism. If we add to miserable pay and lack of safety net the fact that one also misses the social (!) aspect of sharing one's work experience with co-workers, there isn't that much awesomeness left for the sharing micro-entrepreneur. TaskRabbit's CEO Leah Busque once said that the goal of her company was to "revolutionize the world's labor force".[146] Unfortunately, it looks as though Mrs Busque could have it her way – and more so than we should wish for. One doesn't have to agree with Stanley Aronowitz, who refers to the 'gigs' offered the by sharing economy as "wage slavery in which all the cards are held, mediated by technology, by the employer, whether it is the intermediary company or the customer".[147] However, what does become increasingly obvious is that digital platforms represent a formidable instrument for an attack on the achievements of the labour movement – which for very good reasons we consider to be one of the pillars of modern, democratic civilization. What is important to realise in this context is that this has nothing to do with the sharing

146   Tsotsis 2012.
147   Ibid.

economy going off rails or betraying its real spirit. Instead, this is simply the logic of platform capitalism. As Sascha Lobo puts it succinctly in his *Spiegel* blog:

> By controlling their ecosystems, platforms create a stage on which every economic transaction can be turned into an auction. Nothing minimizes cost better than an auction – including the cost of labour. That's why labour is the crucial societal aspect of platform capitalism. It is exactly here that we will have to decide whether to harness the enormous advantages of platform capitalism and the sharing economy or to create a 'dumping market' where the exploited amateurs only have the function to push professional prices down.

For Lobo, the threat of platform capitalism consists in its systematic erosion of professional standards, setting off a price-race to the bottom that translates into an economy where one thing is shared above all: very low income. The *Wall Street Journal*'s Christopher Mims agrees, calling platforms "remarkably efficient machines for producing near minimum-wage jobs". Mims even goes as far as to liken the sharing economy – though in a tongue-in-cheek manner – to a "new feudalism". Historically speaking, he is not too far off the mark. Platform capitalism's technique of controlling market access *vis-à-vis* (in)dependent workers finds its historical predecessor in the "putting-out system" that emerged during the transitional period between feudalism and capitalism proper. The putting-out system was particularly prominent in the 17th and 18th centuries (before the arrival of the factory) and applied above all (but not exclusively) to textile production. Putting-out was an early form of subcontracting, whereby a merchant provided (put-out) raw materials that workers could then process at home, with the help of their wives and children, at flexible hours, on their own machinery. One of the advantages of the putting-out system was that it enabled merchants and workers to circumvent the regulations of the guilds, just as platform capitalism evades today's labour regulations. This worked well for the merchants and sometimes also increased the well-being of the families doing the work, yet often it didn't. This had to do with the fact that the merchant-middlemen were in a position to control both the prices at which raw materials were sold to the petty producers and the prices at which they bought back the finished goods. Cut off from the market, the petty producers were utterly dependent on their merchant, whose enterprise was near risk free. In case of a shrinking market, for instance, a merchant would purchase less product from the producer, which would then mean less income, unpaid debts (for buying equipment or raw material) and so on. Thus, while the merchant capitalists were able to extract risk free, maximum profit, the petty producers remained in a position of proto-feudal serfdom.

I don't want to overstate the historical analogy, but with regard to the position of labour within platform capitalism, the structure of dependency and risk is quite similar to that of the putting-out system.[148] Market access is mediated and controlled by platform operators, while the entrepreneurial risk is completely outsourced to the eventual 'vendor'. To refer to this situation in terms of micro-entrepreneurship is euphemistic to the extent that it ignores the dependency of the 'vendor' with regard to the platform. An entrepreneur is someone who 'undertakes' (from the French *entreprendre*) or begins something new. Since Schumpeter, we understand an entrepreneur to be someone who turns an idea or invention into an innovation to be sold on the market. Doing a range of premeditated chores or filling in as a part-time

---

148 There is talk of car 'sharing' platforms pressuring drivers into buying new cars through shady subprime lenders (Tiku 2014; Smith 2014), so even at the level of unsustainable debt for equipment there is a clear parallel here.

chauffeur is something quite different.[149] More apposite, it seems to me, would be to speak of the emergence of a *platform proletariat*, in the sense of both the material tendency of pauperisation as intended by Marx and the loss of know-how or *savoir-faire* (the ability to create that distinguishes the entrepreneur in the widest sense of the word) that Bernard Stiegler bemoans in his *New Critique of Political Economy*.

Whether intended or not, behind the rhetoric of the sharing economy lurks a project of comprehensive deregulation by digital default, aiming at the proletarianisation of substantial sections of the population. Let us not forget that many of the big players and financiers of platform capitalism are part of Silicon Valley's ideological landscape, whose inflated hippie rhetoric of "making the world a better place" is no more than a thin veneer for its aggressive libertarianism trenched in Randian testosterone. What platform capitalism demonstrates is that we have moved beyond the soft persuasion strategy of the Californian Ideology into a model of open economic warfare against the remnants of the welfare state. What not even decades of neoliberal politics could achieve – the reversal of labour standards to pre-industrial servitude – platform capitalism, if unchecked, might actually accomplish. If Clausewitz called war the continuation of politics by other means, then platform capitalism is the continuation of neoliberal politics by means of economic warfare. We can see this clearly when looking at the actual sustainability and profitability of the business models involved: the enormity of funding financing the rapid global expansion of a company like Uber is not, of course, a sign of its profitability, but a bet on the company's future placed by big capital investors whose political position on market

149   Recently, there have been suggestions to reintroduce the legal position of "dependent contractor" to deal with the insecurities endemic to the new platform proletariat. The issue even entered the 2016 US election campaign. See, eg., Dwyer 2015.

regulation of any kind I don't need to spell out here.[150] If there ever was a reason to revive the dusty notion of class war, this is it. Platform capitalism is class war from above!

6. 'Sharing' Is the Opium of the People

But, many readers will respond, isn't there so much more to the sharing economy than the dire picture painted here suggests? Well, yes and no. As I have stated above, using digital platforms to enable the recirculation of goods or increase the utilisation of durable assets could make consumption more resource efficient and, perhaps, more sustainable as well.[151] However, what platforms of this kind are enabling is reusing and reselling, not sharing. Yes, this can be economically and ecologically advantageous, but again it has nothing to do with sharing or going towards a different economic system.

Then there are the service exchange platforms whose monetised variety sells tickets to the time machine back to the hyperexploitative future of a digitised putting-out system. Yes, there are also time banks and other community based barter systems but – not very surprisingly – they appear to be too clumsy to really take off on a significant scale.

Finally, we might also include the somewhat revived forms of the cooperative, i.e., those initiatives and efforts sharing assets or space for the sake of production, rather than consumption. They are, of course, far from new, but today often come in all sorts of shapes and hybrids, such as hacker, maker and coworking spaces. The problem with these neo-cooperatives is that wherever they

150   In China, where Uber is having great difficulties at the moment, the company burns about US$1 Billion annually in an attempt to subsidise its way into the enormous market. See Lacey 2015.

151   AirBnB would be the notorious counterexample here as its effects are increasingly making city life unsustainable.

were able to scale, they also lost their initial sharing impetus in order to become commercial platforms.[152]

Thus, a sober assessment of the sharing economy suggests that sharing in any meaningful sense is an absolutely marginal phenomenon here. And this is exactly why I suggested dropping the term altogether. In no way is it possible to remove the ideological toxicity from the notion of the sharing economy, simply because it is too valuable an ethical smokescreen to not be picked up by the marketeers of platform capitalism. Take Rachel Botsman, who was a consultant to GE and IBM before becoming the queen of the sharing economy. In her book, *What's Mine is Yours*, the first standard reference for anyone who wanted to learn about the sharing economy, Botsman set the tone for what would become the sharing debate. One of her central claims was that collaborative consumption enables people

> to realize the enormous benefits of access to products and services over ownership, and at the same time save money, space, and time; make friends; and become an active citizen once again.[153]

This is a wonderful statement, as it reveals the veritable intellectual evil that is the *modus operandi* of some of the so-called thought leaders of sharing. While the argument regarding "access over ownership", etc. has some empirical validity, and the reference to "making friends" might be admissible for a minor section of the sharing economy (think couch surfing or the local tool 'library'), slipping in "active citizens" is simply the opposite of intellectual integrity. In a very cunning move, Botsman managed to create the ethical charge for platform capitalism that it needs in order to operate under the label of sharing economy.

152 For the case of coworking, I have tried to demonstrate this in Chapter 3.
153 Botsman 2010: XV-XVI.

Botsman, however, is by no means the worst of the pack. John Zimmer, co-founder of *Lyft*, told *Wired* writer Jason Tanz some time ago that the sharing economy bestows on us the gift of a revived community spirit. Referring to his visit to the Oglala Sioux reservation, he writes:

> Their sense of community, of connection to each other and to their land, made me feel more happy and alive than I've ever felt. We now have the opportunity to use technology to help us get there.

Even in a time when outlets such as *Wired* work hard on lowering the intellectual standards of its readership, one cannot help but be shocked at the frivolity of this comparison. Of course, Zimmer is on a marketing mission here, and this is also exactly what one would expect of him. Yet, the problem is that due to the nature of what might be called the epistemological milieu around the sharing economy, statements of this kind have become common currency – in spite of Scholz's hopeful statement to the contrary at the beginning of this chapter. They seamlessly connect to a network of similar claims that, taken together, form a mesh of half-truths, unsubstantiated beliefs and feel-good claims against which the sword of reason is all but powerless.

It is in the context of this climate of ideological distortion created around platform capitalism that we have to assess scholarly accounts of the sharing economy, such as *Debating the Sharing Economy* by the great Amercian sociologist of labour, Juliet Schor. Although Schor is quite aware of what she calls the "dark side" of the sharing economy, she resolutely expresses her belief in the "sharing movement" in terms of making an important contribution to a perceived social transition to a small-scale, ecologically sustainable economy:

> There is potential in this sector for creating new businesses that allocate value more fairly, that are more democratically organized, that reduce eco-footprints, and that can bring people together in new ways. That is why there has been so much excitement about the sharing economy.[154]

True, "there is potential" but certainly not in the sharing economy. Given the marginalised position of initiatives and projects experimenting with digital technology in order to reinvent models of cooperation and indeed, sharing, the notion that the sharing economy will somehow lead into a social transition is simply delusional. Again, exploring how technologies and the cultures surrounding them can contribute to different modes of organisation for our economies and societies is a fundamental challenge of our time, but the sharing economy does not provide in any way the appropriate platform for these kinds of endeavours. Schor's great examples of transitional activities in the name of the sharing economy, such as the Parisian OuiShare festival or sharing city initiatives that have spread around the globe, are much more ambivalent in their intention and outcome than she would like to admit. The same goes for the Buen Conocer project that set out to reimagine the Ecuadorian society "according to principles of sharing — open networks, open production, and an economy of the commons"[155] under the direction of the P2P Foundation. As Schor's article demonstrates, the spectacular failure of the project has not prevented a manicured version of the story (minus the failure part) to become staple of the sharing economy's mythology.

There can be no doubt that the marketeers of platform capitalism will continue to exploit the label 'sharing economy' to mask

154   Schor 2014: 11.
155   Ibid.: 1–2.

its true ambitions. What should prevent them from doing so? However, this also means that those who continue to promote the sharing economy as if it was a valid path toward a more democratic, participatory and egalitarian economy are not just delusional but also complicit in platform capitalism's obvious reactionary tendencies. For those who are engaging in experiments around peer-to-peer or neo-cooperative production regimes, the task regarding the sharing economy is quite clear: get out of it! If you want to be more than the ethical charger of a class war from above, you'll have to put a significant distance between you and the ideological outlets of platform capitalism.

7. When Exodus is a Sagacious Act

Thus herein lies the sagacity when dealing with platform capitalism: a resolute exodus from the euphemistic rhetoric and institutions of the sharing economy. All too often, the well-meaning public and academic discourse around sharing and collaboration are driven by the techgnostic belief in the healing nature of digital technology. Juliet Schor is absolutely right when she states: "technologies are only as good as the political and social context in which they are employed."[156] At the moment, the political and juridical regulation of platform capitalism is only beginning. For those of us who truly believe that "sharing is caring", it is an enormously important task to stop contributing to the confusion wilfully created by those who *own* stakes in the sharing economy. This is not just a challenge we face *vis-à-vis* our political decision makers who need to understand that letting the economy regress to pre-capitalist modes of exploitation has absolutely nothing to do with innovative politics. It is also a responsibility we carry with regard to the generation of young professionals and freelancers

156 Ibid.: 12.

who are regularly fed the notion that not being paid properly for their labour makes them the avant-garde of a better economic system to come. The truth of the matter, as Nathan Schneider puts it on *Aljazeera America*, is that

> the sharing sector of the conventional economy built on venture capital and exploited labor is a multibillion dollar business, while the idea of a real sharing economy based on cooperatives, worker solidarity and democratic governance remains too much of an afterthought. If the sharing movement really wants to disrupt economic injustice, these should be its first priorities.

I hope that it has become clear over the course of this chapter that it is in no way the intention of the sharing economy to "disrupt economic injustice". The sharing economy does not exist. Or, in the words of *Slate*'s business writer Matthew Yglesias: "This is a dumb term, and it deserves to die". Again, this is not to say that there are no great initiatives and indeed businesses that are trying to use the power of digital technology or simply their imagination to practice forms of exchange that could actually be called sharing. They do exist and it is wonderful that they do. However, their value in the context of the current sharing economy is that of an illegitimate ethical charge, a fig leaf for an alarming mutation of our economy. I think they deserve better! Yet, in order to even have a chance to turn this development into a serendipitous exploration of the encounter of digital technology and economic organisation for the sake of fairer, more democratic practices, what we need to do right now is to be clear about the indisputable fact that platform capitalism does not equal the sharing economy at all.

VII University as *Übungsraum*
Notes on HE's Creative Transformation 157

1.Serendipity and the Long Shadow of Black Mountain

It is no accident that in the summer of 2015, the *Deutsche National-galerie* in Berlin put on a show dedicated to Black Mountain College, the legendary North Carolina art school that influenced the trajectory of Modernism in the second half of the 20th century perhaps more than any other institution. The list of names of students or teachers populating this exceptional place between 1933 and 1957 reads like a Who's Who of 20th century art and design and, perhaps to a lesser extent, of the natural and social sciences as well. And yet, the show didn't focus much on the great names or the famous works they produced. It did not dwell on Buckminster Fuller's invention of the geodesic dome there, or the school's importance for the development of abstract expressionism, or the impact of the collaboration between Merce Cunningham and John Cage on contemporary art. Instead, the exhibition demonstrated the college's appeal as an educational institution, built on an ethos of radically democratic interdisciplinarity, experimentation and exploration. Initially, it was not even conceived as an art school *per se*, but rather as a free educational institution where young men and women could develop the knowledge and skills that suited them best in their quest to make a meaningful

157   An earlier version of this chapter appeared in Comunian, Roberta & Gilmore, Abigail (2016) *Higher Education and the Creative Economy: Beyond the Campus,* London Routledge

contribution to society. As the show's curators, Eugen Blume and Gabriele Knapstein, write in the exhibition catalogue:

> Black Mountain College has remained an exemplary institution to the present day and, particularly in our time of higher education reforms, which posit principles of economic efficiency as the sole measure of success, it is a counter-example of direct democratic praxis.[158]

Much like the Bauhaus, from which many of its members migrated, Black Mountain College presents something of an ideal type of Higher Education (HE) that in the early 21st century we seem to have completely lost touch with. True, Black Mountain College operated on a very small, intimate scale, with little more than a hundred students enrolled at its peak. From the point of view of those involved in running today's massive educational machines, this must sound like pure luxury. Yet, at a time when university administrations throughout the Western world make claims as to their commitment to innovation and creativity, one wonders why these 'commitments' tend to have such detrimental effects on the material conditions of research and learning.

For France's most eminent philosopher, Michel Serres, the problem is fairly obvious: universities are increasingly failing the young generations because of their clinging to obsolete disciplinary structures. What our institutions of HE fail to realise, Serres writes in his *Petite Poucette*, is the revolutionary potential inherent in digital technology that offers a great opportunity for a radical rethinking of the university. With all the knowledge of the world available at the tap of a finger, he argues, universities have an immense opportunity to reinvent themselves. They can become institutions of transdisciplinarity, shifting the function of education from knowledge transmission to teaching students

158   Blume et al. 2015: 14.

skills to enable them to creatively explore the serendipitous connections between the bodies of knowledge previously confined to their disciplines, but which now are carried around in most pockets via smartphones and other mobile devices. In other words, massive student populations are no excuse for their regulation via disciplinary structures and constraints; on the back of digital technology, it has again become possible to climb the Black Mountain – not just for future artists but for everyone.

This chapter takes Michel Serres' intervention as its point of departure for a reflection on the current challenges to HE in terms of providing a space where the younger generation is able to acquire the skills and capabilities they need in order to make a meaningful contribution to society. Universities are the infrastructural organs where society conceives of and develops important elements of its possible futures across the different academic disciplines. It is here that society's capacity to invent and innovate in the future is determined. Given the rapidly changing social environment, the question of the right skills and opportunities in today's HE presents a formidable challenge.

In order to do justice to the fundamental nature of this question, this chapter starts from a philosophical point of view and, for most of its part, will also stay at this level of analysis. It does not aim, however, to be an exercise in detached philosophising. The reason why Serres' line of argument makes for an interesting point of departure is that it provides the philosophical substantiation for the so-called creative industries programmes that have been introduced by university administrations across Europe and elsewhere. The creative industries makeover within the disciplines considered relevant to this field (Arts & Humanities, some Social Sciences, as well as Design and parts of Technology Education) tries not only to overcome disciplinary boundaries within academia, but also to connect learning and research to the relevant professional fields beyond the university. Multi-, inter- and transdisciplinarity are important catchwords for these efforts, but also, and perhaps even more importantly, serendipity. Creative industries programmes, collaborations, and campuses are seen as platforms enabling disciplinary and institutional transgression that can reproduce, in a timely fashion, the serendipitous encounters that gave an institution like Black Mountain College its enormous creative and innovative edge.

Both for Serres and the proponents of creative industries education, serendipity has become a guiding reference with regard to the reorganisation of the university. The danger here is that these analytical and practical efforts are guided by a vague buzzword that can mean anything to anyone (we've seen the same thing occurring with creativity, innovation, social innovation, etc.). Within creative industries discourse, sagacity tends to be strictly understood in terms of entrepreneurial agility: the accidental encounter with an idea, an artefact, a technology, a specific approach, or a skill that is quickly transformed into a product or service. To be able to facilitate this sagacity is clearly of great value; however, one wonders if there aren't other rationales and logics of creativity that HE can cater to as well. To explore this question, I turn to Richard Sennett's analysis of the crafts(wo)man's virtuosity – which he understands in an immediately political sense in terms of the question of social participation and in the final analysis of citizenship.

While Sennett's reflection on the political implications of virtuosity helps widen our view on what it means to be 'creative', we need to bring this question back – rather literally – to the space of HE. Here, the work of German philosopher Peter Sloterdijk is instructive, as it turns the Foucauldian critique of discipline into a celebration of *Übung* (literally: exercise or training). According to Sloterdijk, who speaks with a clear Nietzschean accent here, the human being is an *Übungswesen*, i.e., a creature that needs exercise or training to grow into and beyond itself. *Übung*, of course, requires space and the task of providing such space, or indeed *Übungsraum*, is exactly that of HE. With reference to Sloterdijk, one might say that traditionally the challenge for HE has been to create a nexus where the relevant kind of *Übung* finds its appropriate *Raum*. Today, one of the areas in which this challenge needs to be readdressed is in the context of the creative industries and HE: How to integrate the creative industries as a platform for serendipity in an *Übungsraum* that values vocational skill within a comprehensive ethos of *Bildung*?

2. Of Thumbs and Heads: Damned to be Intelligent?

Michel Serres' *Petite Poucette* is a strange little book. Written as a "love letter to the networked generation" (the subtitle of the German translation), it celebrates the digital savviness of his grandchildren and their peers. *Petite Poucette* is the French name of Hans Christian Andersen's Thumbelina, a Danish fairytale character that was inspired by the much older English folk character Tom Thumb. The title is thus a pun on the agility with which the fingers of the Millennials dash over the touch screens of their mobile devices. For Serres, *Petite Poucette* does not just stand for a new generation, but represents a new kind of human being. While the exact circumstances of her coming into being remain in the dark, whatever gave birth to her had something to do with digital technology. To illustrate what is going on, Serres refers to Jacques de Voragine's *Golden Legend*, that tells the story of St. Dionysius, the first bishop of Paris who was captured by the Roman army and sentenced to death by beheading on top of what was later to be called Montmartre. Half way to the top, the lazy soldiers decide to avoid the strenuous ascent and cut off his head on the spot. The bishop's head drops to the ground. Miraculously, though, the decapitated St. Dionysius raises, grabs his head, and continues his ascent – head in hands. The soldiers flee in shock and horror. The point Serres is trying to make here is that today *Petite Poucette* is holding her head in her hands as well. She is decapitated in the sense of having her intellectual, cognitive capabilities externalised into devices whose memory is thousands of times more powerful than hers. Which leads Serres to the question:

> What then is it that we keep on carrying on our shoulders after being decapitated? Renewed and living intuition. Being 'canned' [in the computer, SO], pedagogy releases us to the pure pleasure of invention. Great: Are we damned to become intelligent? [159]

And here is where Serres sees the main problem with HE institutions: they are unable or unwilling to adjust to this new empty-headed yet agile-thumbed generation that does not need knowledge as stock anymore (as it always has it at hand anyway), but needs knowledge as process that feeds intuition, invention, and innovation.

Serres goes on to present his ideas on what could be done to turn the university into a place that would be more accommodating to the evolutionary advances of Tom Thumb and *Petite Poucette*. He introduces another historical analogy, again from Paris, yet this time closer to the present. It concerns Boucicaut, founder of one of the world's first department stores, Le Bon Marché. Émile Zola made Boucicaut the template for Octave Mouret, the hero of his novel *Au Bonheur des Dames*. At one point in the novel, Mouret, following a whim, abandons the well-ordered, classified structure of his department store, turning it into a labyrinth where the shopping-crazed dames find the latest silk-fashions (we are talking about the mid-19th century) next to fresh vegetables, etc. The resulting chaos that his move generated was an instant success: sales went through the roof. For Serres, this provides a

---

159   Serres 2012: 55.

great metaphor for what has to happen at universities. They can learn, he argues, from Boucicaut's principle of serendipity, the principle of the unsought discovery through unexpected encounters. The university needs a reform that mobilises the disparate against classification. "The disparate", as the author puts it, "has advantages that reason cannot even dream of." [160]

The reference to serendipity is crucial here. On the face of it, it rearticulates, as a philosophical gesture, the call for disciplinary and institutional transgression that re-emerges on the back of the development of digital technology and creative industries. This is not wrong *per se*: it does make a lot of sense to think about disciplinary transgression for the sake of serendipity when it comes to keeping HE in sync with the development and requirements of its social environment. Where the arguments of both Serres and the proponents of the creative industries HE-makeover derail, however, is when they judge the significance of serendipity to HE only in terms defined by supply and demand, by the market rather than criteria based on the intrinsic value of knowledge gleaned from serendipitous encounter and exchange. Isn't it curious that Serres believes the department store to be the apposite metaphor for his call for disciplinary transgression, rather than, say, the much richer and more relevant historical examples of institutions such as Black Mountain College or the Bauhaus? And doesn't his attempt to rethink HE on the template of the Le Bon Marché correspond to the fascination with the 'serendipitous' business models of Silicon Valley often held by the proponents of the creative industries approach to HE?

The point to be made here is that such an understanding of serendipity as disciplinary transgression for the sake of market success is an extremely narrow one. Whenever academic institutions in the past were successfully working on the principle of

160   Serres 2012: 44.

serendipity (as were those quoted above) they explicitly avoided such constraint. These institutions were serendipitous precisely because of their comprehensive practice of disciplinary transgression. Wouldn't it be rather nonsensical to argue for a disciplinary opening in order to then frame this opening in the narrow parameters of supply and demand? Even Silicon Valley, whose current business models function according to very impoverished interpretations of serendipity, the expected encounter between a great start-up idea and a willing investor would not exist without the serendipitous encounter of post-war cybernetic research and Sixties hippie culture, both of which were not exactly streamlined business cultures.[161] What this shows is that serendipity can and should be an important reference with regard to a timely reorganisation of HE, but only if it is taken seriously in its own right, rather than preformatted by the logic of market exchange. The department store has obviously lost its power of attraction, but, as I said in the prologue, there is also more to serendipity than meets the Google-glassed eye.

As I repeatedly argue throughout this book, there are two dimensions to serendipity – accident and sagacity – and these two dimensions have their specific articulations within the context of HE as well. With regard to the accidental encounter, the diversity of elements encountering each other is crucial for the generation of novelty. Here, we find the inspiration for Serres' argument about the jumbling of university departments as a way of "mobilising the disparate against classification".[162] What Serres might not appreciate is that universities all over Europe have for some time been investigating the creative industries as models for inspiration and 'best practice' in 'creating synergies' and facilitating unexpected encounters. It is true that interdisciplinarity

161 See Chapter 5.
162 Serres 2012: 43.

had become an issue for HE long before the creative industries became a policy instrument. However, the influence of creative industries discourse, particularly on the academic management of the arts and humanities as well as some of the social sciences, has substantially modified the discussion of interdisciplinarity. An important source of inspiration for the creative reorganisation of HE is now found in those emphatically creative and innovative spaces, hubs, and incubators that make up a crucial part of our so-called creative cities. The problem here is that often universities seem strangely to lack the critical faculties to properly assess these 'best practices', and their relationship to creative learning and entrepreneurship. As it turns out – and this goes very much against the grain of popular myth – in terms of their populations, these places often display the very homogeneity that the philosopher criticises with regard to the university. In Amsterdam, this has recently led to a debate on "creative ghettos", questioning the sensibility of spatial policies where creative producers remain largely among themselves.[163] One might indeed wonder whether the spatialities of the creative industries, and the corresponding creative class, are the right source of inspiration (or even method) when it comes to reforming HE – even in terms of their supposed creative diversity. Just think of the ubiquity of the demand of 'like-mindedness' as a precondition for collaboration in the creative industries scenes. And let us also not forget that there is a veritable army of coaches and experts that have besieged the creative class, radically streamlining their ability to creatively express themselves in the name of entrepreneurial success. This is not to diminish the various impulses that have emerged from the sector in terms of urban development or new business models. However, the mobilisation of "the disparate against classification" that we see in the creative city and business is of an entirely different

163 Vonk 2014; Cnossen & Olma 2014.

order than what is needed in today's university. Let me repeat, what is at stake here is the kind of inter-, multi- or transdisciplinarity that cannot be bound by the straightjacket of the market.

And this, then, becomes indeed a question of the second dimension of serendipity, i.e., sagacity. In the Introduction, I defined sagacity in terms of defiance or, indeed, resistance, as an engagement with the potentially new in such a way as to open up ruling regimes of knowledge and power to the possibility of future deviation. Such an understanding of sagacity in the context of serendipity would allow us to broaden the creative industries approach to academic inter-, multi-, and transdisciplinarity that today is overly focused on entrepreneurial and technological skills. These are important skills, but need to be integrated within a pedagogic culture, encouraging the young to question the present for the sake of finding their own way to contribute to a desirable future as an act of self-determination.

Adopting a broader perspective on the purpose of HE is far from revolutionary. The ambition to educate not just disciplinary specialists, but sovereign individuals capable of participating in and contributing to society as active citizens, has always been part and parcel of HE's ethos. It is only recently that the neoliberal disdain for anything public has gripped our institutions of HE to the extent that this important dimension of education has been wilfully left to rot.[164] If today, our romantic gaze is going back to institutions such as Black Mountain College or Bauhaus, this is because these institutions based their innovative capacity on a pedagogical ethos that treated creativity and citizenship as two sides of the same coin.

Serendipity has a role to play in our efforts to redesign our universities as places of creativity and innovation. However, it should

164   Collini 2012, for instance, provides a critical reflection on the British situation as well as a polemic on the question *What Are Universities For?*

be the serendipity of the comprehensively sagacious kind, not the one of the quick buck. And this means that we have to rethink the relationship between creativity and citizenship for HE as well. I am aware this is a difficult question, particularly in a country like the UK, where HE has effectively become a question of supply and demand. Yet, while one cannot naïvely ignore the reality of the neoliberal university, it would be irresponsible to pragmatically accept the current dysfunctionality of HE. For those of us who believe in education as a generational responsibility towards the young, the normative question of comprehensive *Bildung* needs to remain the ethical horizon. And even for those of us who are of a more purely economic or business persuasion, it should be clear that the market can never generate the diversity of input necessary for truly path-breaking innovation.[165]

3. Virtuosity: Rethinking *Bildung* between Creativity and Citizenship

Richard Sennett has addressed the question of *Bildung* precisely in terms of the relationship between creativity (creative labour) and citizenship. In order to do this, Sennett engages in a historical analysis of craftsmanship as virtuosity. Virtuosity is relevant to this context because, as outlined below, it entertains an interesting relation to the notion of sagacity. It is in the contemporary mutations of the traditional practice of virtuosity that I hope to find the means for a further conceptual refinement of sagacity (and sagacious serendipity) that will allow us to creatively rethink HE, without falling into the trap of ideological complicity.

Sennett's *The Craftsman* is an attack on the classical liberal

---

165 Often, the market cannot even generate the necessary funding for the research required for substantial product innovation, as Marina Mazzucato's brilliant book *The Entrepreneurial State* shows – even and above all for famous Silicon Valley companies like Apple.

position according to which craftsmanship is a mere economic matter. From the classical liberal point of view, the craftsman is the *bourgeois*, the economic citizen, and as such qualitatively different from the *citoyen*, the political citizen proper, so to speak. Sennett challenges this dichotomy by arguing that craftsmanship is an institutional practice connecting the worlds of *bourgeois* and *citoyen*. As he demonstrates, craftsmanship, as the result of a process of dedicated apprenticeship, provides a crucial training ground for faculties that are indispensable for a meaningful practice of citizenship. This is how he summarises his argument:

> The argument ... is that the craft of making physical things provides insights into the techniques of experience that can shape our dealings with others. Both the difficulties and the possibilities of making things well apply to making human relationships. Material challenges like working with resistance or managing ambiguity are instructive in understanding the resistance people harbor to one another or the uncertain boundaries between people. ... [W]ho we are arises directly from what our bodies can do. Social consequences are built into the structure and the functioning of the human body, as in the workings of the human hand. I argue no more and no less than that the capacities our bodies have to shape physical things are the same capacities we draw on in social contacts.[166]

Sennett's central concept here is virtuosity. The virtuosity of the craftsman, i.e., the purposeful application of one's body to the shaping of objects, Sennett understands as the precondition for the virtuosity of the citizen in shaping social relations with his/her fellow citizens. The experience of making a unique contribution through one's engagement with matter generates the

166   Sennett 2008: 289-290.

self-consciousness necessary for a meaningful participation in society.[167] What Sennett describes here is a process of formation of individual sovereignty in the sense of professional virtuosity as being the path toward the ability for meaningful participation in society, i.e., political virtuosity. This conception of virtuosity necessitates a continuum that connects the professional skill of the craftsman to the political skill of the citizen. Of course, with regard to the challenges HE is facing today, Sennett's emphasis on the physical nature of education seems slightly outdated; in order to think through virtuosity in terms that resonate with our contemporary situation (in general, as well as HE in particular), the notion needs to be opened out.

This can be done with the help of German philosopher Peter Sloterdijk. His *Du Musst Dein Leben Ändern* approaches the question of education in terms of the Greek notion of *áskēsis*, the original meaning of which is exercise or training. Sloterdijk's exploration of *áskēsis* fundamentally builds on Foucault's excavation of the relation between discipline and citizenship, but rejects its reduction to a dark, manipulative, and somewhat illegitimate force. Rather than Foucault's prisons and places of repressive surveillance, Sloterdijk sees the institutions of the Christian-humanist discipline as providing modernity with the space for the essential formation of the citizenry. It's the strict schools and universities, the craftsmen's workshops and artistic studios that institutionalise disciplinary asceticism as a dialectical process of self-formation in relation to the formative structures (the moulds) of society. Provocative as he likes to be, Sloterdijk here speaks of spaces for "human orthopaedics", the result of which are generations of "virtuosi" clearing the path and leading the way

---

167 This, of course, is John Dewey's (1938) pragmatist philosophy of education in a (very small) nutshell that also served as a guide to the experiment of Black Mountain College as well.

in Europe's "journey into the age of the arts and techniques".[168]

The virtuosi who Sloterdijk understands as the (never quite finished) products of such orthopaedics are human beings able to lead their lives autonomously precisely because they have gone through the formative process of asceticism. What Sloterdijk's celebration of asceticism demonstrates is that virtuosity, as the result of *Übung*, is not exclusively linked to the physicality of traditional craftsmanship in Sennett's sense, but applies generally to human beings, in so far as they are *Übungswesen* (i.e., creatures that need exercise or training in order to grow into themselves). And while the standards of the Christian-humanist discipline have run their course as exclusive ethical parameters of education, the question should be exactly what kind of ethos should replace them.

Sennett, unfortunately, is unable to address this question in a timely fashion. The merit of his argument lies in having made explicit the connection between craftsmanship and citizenship in terms of a continuum of virtuosity. Also, his critique of the rapid devaluation of craftsmanship, as a result of neoliberal politics, cannot be easily dismissed. However, Sennett's main problem is that his argument is too romantic to offer any possible way out of this predicament; yearning for pedagogical methods that are both unsustainable in the age of mass education and largely useless for today's Tom Thumbs and *Petite Poucettes*. The virtuosity necessary to manoeuvre today's economic as well as social, technological, and political terrain seems to be quite different from the one Sennett has in mind.[169] It cannot belong to the bygone era of crafting. Neither is it the virtuosity of the factory and the office – if such thing ever existed. It is a new kind of virtuosity

168   Sloterdijk 2009: 497.

169   For three different versions of this difference see Boltanski & Chiapello 1999; Friebe & Lobo 2006; Stiegler 2014b.

that necessarily entails the ability to reconstruct the continuum connecting a professional ethos appropriate to the digital era with the social responsibility of a sovereign political subject.

4. Virtuosity, Sagacity and the Need for *Übungsraum*

This new kind of virtuosity is not going to emerge by itself. Universities, as the infrastructural organs where society conceives of and develops important elements of its possible futures, are responsible for the construction of Sennett's continuum between economic professionalism and social and political participation. Having ignored this responsibility is as much an unforgivable omission of Serres' book, as it is the root cause of the crisis of the neoliberal university: HE is taken to be a machine whose purpose is the commercial organisation of knowledge transfer. Since all the knowledge today is canned in the memory of computers and digital networks, thumbs have become more important than heads. Yet, this kind of knowledge has very little to do with virtuosity or, indeed, sagacity. Rather, it is close to what Bernard Stiegler in his *States of Shock* calls *bêtise*, or stupidity. Limiting the question of knowledge to that of technological savviness and entrepreneurial skill – as Serres and the proponents of the creative industries in the academy at least implicitly do – reduces human beings to functional extensions of a technological system; ignoring the crucial importance of *savoir-vivre*, knowledge of how to live and love. The question is: How can universities that are themselves in a state of profound disorientation become institutions of care, where Generation Y can get the tools, skills, and, indeed, the knowledge to leave their stupidity behind in order to become sagacious virtuosi of their own lives?

To even begin addressing this question, we need to move the notion of virtuosity even closer to the present, which, in our context, means closer to sagacity and serendipity. The work of the

Italian philosopher Paolo Virno is instructive here, as it diagnoses the emergence of a new and very different kind of virtuosity that is linked to the immaterialisation of economy and society. Immaterialisation refers to the process by which the immaterial dimension of products, i.e. their symbolic, aesthetic and social value, increasingly outweigh their classical material dimension. Images, knowledge, information, codes, affects, as well as social relationships *per se*, have become the predominant factors in determining the value a particular commodity has on the market. In other words, for Virno, immaterialisation stands for what policy makers and economists try to articulate in terms of digitisation and creative industries.

In Virno's interpretation, this immaterialisation of economic practice leads to a development that seems to be the opposite of what Sennett describes: rather than virtuosity disappearing due to the growing distance between labour and politics, the virtuosity of labour and that of politics begin to converge. As commodities, as well as the ways in which they are produced, become increasingly cultural, communicational, semiotic, expressive, and so on, the sphere of production takes on many of the characteristics that were traditionally assigned to the world of politics. Today, production, distribution, and consumption are predicated on a techno-cultural infrastructure enabling constant multidimensional flows of communication. This is to say that today's regime of production runs on techno-cultural platforms sustaining 'publicly' organised spaces that in a strange manner resemble those of politics. The virtuosity required by this new spatiality is one that is immediately and radically social. It implies the permanent presence of others as co-producers, co-distributors, and co-consumers. So the new virtuosity is intrinsically relational and often involves even performative dimensions.

For Virno, this new kind of virtuosity marks a moment in the development of the human species in which our basic socio-linguistic faculties, the human ability to creatively communicate, have become productive. Robert Reich highlighted this fact more than twenty years ago in his book *The Work of Nations*, where he wrote about the growing importance of so-called "symbolic analysts" within the economy. Since then, the spectrum of activity that applies virtuosity for the sake of generating economic value has expanded massively. From the growing sector of services with (at least) a smile to the experience-creating creative industries, a kind of public space re-emerges, although one in which potentially emancipative, proto-political practice is perpetually transformed into intensified labour.[170]

And here we encounter the point at which virtuosity, in the sense that both Sloterdijk and Sennett understand it, becomes utterly devoid of any political impetus. If the generation of economic value today takes place in a proto-political arena of instant communicative presence and connection, there is an increasing danger for the *citoyen* to collapse into the figure of a comprehensive *bourgeois*, for whom the practice of citizenship perverts into a mere marketing exercise. The creative industries are a great case in point here: just think about the ubiquity of vacuous references to 'community' when addressing customers and clients.

Seen in the light of Virno's critical socio-philosophy, the current attempt to modernise the relevant parts of HE by putting them at the service of the creative industries appears to be an attempt to save a kind of virtuosity that no longer deserves saving. "Let's look at the maker, hacker, and coworking spaces, the Fablabs and creative hubs of the creative city", says the innovation consultant to the university administrator, "and see if we can transfer their timely creativity and innovativeness into the structure of the institution." This is not entirely wrong, but it expresses a skewed perspective. The challenge for the university is not to make

170 This issue is discussed more extensively in Chapter 4.

students more innovative and creative – whatever that might actually mean – but to enable them to manoeuvre the emergent social and economic topology as relatively sovereign individuals, i.e., not just as entrepreneurial *bourgeois* but also as critical *citoyen*. It seems to me that the model of the creative entrepreneur falls as short of this challenge as Serres' reference to Boucicaut's serendipitous department store in *Au Bonheur des Dames*.

5. Higher Education as *Übungsraum* for Social Innovation

Instead, we have to understand, following Sloterdijk, that the human being as *Übungswesen* needs the university as *Übungsraum*, catering actively to the timely reconstruction of the continuum of virtuosity. *Übung macht den Meister* goes the German proverb, and the kind of *Übung* required today is that which not only "makes the master craftsman", but also generates sagacity as a crucial prerequisite to the serendipitous disruption of current cultural and economic templates.

There is indeed, in Zola's novel, a lesson for our times, but it is one that is quite different from what Serres makes of it. By focusing on the serendipity anecdote, what seems to have escaped the philosopher is that Zola's book in its entirety can be read as a commentary on the question of how to engage with emerging cultural and commercial infrastructures, such as today's Internet/digital technology. Zola's *Au Bonheur des Dames* is above all the story of Denise Baudu, a young country girl who comes to Paris with her younger brothers and ends up working as a saleswoman at the department store that lends the novel its title. Her uncle is the owner of a fashion shop across the road from Au Bonheur that, like many other traditional businesses of its kind, is dying thanks to the rapid success and expansion of the great new department store. Thus, Denise's life in Paris unfolds, as it were, at the interface of the old and the new commercial infrastructures. As a saleswoman, she suffers the hardship of a super-exploited employee, but also looks at what is happening in the world of commerce with great interest and analytical appreciation. She has an unusual understanding of the contemporary processes of socio-economic change, yet she doesn't allow herself to be overwhelmed and captured by them.

The integrity she displays amid this great transformation is also metaphorically played out in the love story that unfolds between her and Mouret, the owner of Au Bonheur. Mouret plays the role of the great seducer, not only with regard to the masses of (mostly) female clients his store attracts but also in his private life. He is the smooth operator who seduces his victims for the sake of his business as well as his pleasure. He is, in a way, the bodily extension of Au Bonheur des Dames, his great machine of seduction. Denise falls in love with him yet resists his advances until the very end when he has to concede that the only way to 'get her' is in fact to take her as his wife. True, there is a somewhat tedious moralism to Zola's story, but this is not what interests me presently. The lesson, I think, that can be taken from the story of Denise is that even if one is immersed in a new and overwhelming techno-cultural infrastructure, one does not need to submit to the logic of the new machine. The reason why Denise survives and eventually even thrives in the rapidly changing environment of 1860s Paris, is that she doesn't allow herself to be seduced by the new cultural and economic techniques and technologies. Again, it isn't that she doesn't want to keep up with the times or that she rejects novelty; rather, she looks for modes of engagement that allow her to meet the emerging machine of seduction on her own terms. Sure, there is little leeway for someone like her, but whenever there is, she recognises it and makes the effort.

And this is, I believe, where the challenge lies for our contemporary educational institutions. Rather than mystifying the technological advances of the Internet and expect the generation of digital natives to somehow come to grips with its challenges, we need modes of education that enable young minds to not only performatively but also critically and, indeed, defiantly, engage with today's rapid technological progress. Technological savviness is a precondition, but is by no means the end of it. Our schools and universities need to become institutions where critical analytical capabilities for the digital age are cultivated. I essentially agree with Bernard Stiegler here, who understands this in terms of society's obligation to care for its younger generations.

To create the necessary *Übungsraum*, or training spaces, we need a new wave of social innovation that liberates our educational institutions from their docility and opportunism. Here, the reference to social innovation is in no way intended as an endorsement of the homonymous policy discourse. This conceptually confused and ideologically preformatted field of social innovation policy is part and parcel of the neoliberal charade of changeless change, as discussed in Chapter 2. What is meant here by the term 'social innovation' is a collective effort, in the present context requiring the collaboration of teachers, students, parents, and everyone else concerned about the current state of HE to halt the purposeful neoliberal destruction of an essential pillar of our public infrastructure.

The problem, of course, goes much deeper than the supposed lack of disciplinary transgression. There are blatant democratic and economic deficits at our institutions of HE (although they obviously vary between countries) that make even the most basic academic work increasingly impossible, let alone the creation of conditions for meaningful experiment and exploration, i.e. what in the past was referred to as academic freedom. As John Andrew Rice, founder of Black Mountain College, remarked (with a considerable dash of pathos): "Students can be educated for freedom only by teachers who are themselves free."[171] Today, at a time of chronic underpay and short-term contracts on the one hand, and student indebtedness on the other, there is not much freedom left on either side of the equation.

Michel Serres' intervention is unhelpful in this respect. In fact, with his mixture of euphoria for and ignorance of current developments in technology, he might fit well with those academic management bodies that helplessly embrace every digital fashion for the sake of appearing modern. Unfortunately, this is often the chief reason why the creative industries are invoked and, indeed, invited into the university: as another simulation of change, a fig leaf under which the market-Stalinism of neoliberal management can proceed as planned. Much of what creative industries policies stand for amounts to little more than the celebration of apps and entrepreneurship, which suggests that it is a programme leading the Millennials straight into what Bernard Stiegler's *New Critique of Political Economy* calls "digital proletarianisation", that is, the loss of *savoir-vivre*, which also means the loss of critical faculties, and, in the final analysis, the loss of the individual sovereignty that is required for meaningful participation in society. No one is "damned to become intelligent". We cannot let ourselves off the hook so easily.

So perhaps then, Serres is right about the younger generation holding their heads in their hands today. Good education means enabling our students to put their heads back on. However, it is unlikely that current university management will take steps in this direction out of their own accord. The kind of social innovation needed lies with university occupations and student protests like those that in the summer of 2015 spread from Amsterdam to universities all over Europe. Here, we saw, for the duration of a few weeks, the emergence of a timely *Übungsraum* for the

---

171   Blume et. al. 2015. This is quoted on the backflip of the catalogue.

skills that are necessary to liberate the university from the grip of managerial confusion, as the first step toward the construction of a new university. What this new university is going to look like remains to be seen. What is clear, however, is that academics have the responsibility to support these initiatives of real social innovation whenever they flare up by being part of them. By lending them the little bit of sagacity we have left, we might help turn these initiatives into a serendipitous process: one, at whose end, we will have found something better than we seem to be able to hope for today.

Conclusion

1. In Defence of Serendipity

Serendipity must be defended! If writing this book has taught me anything, it is the urgency with which this statement rings today. It has also become more clear to me, and hopefully to the reader as well, that defending serendipity means removing the ideological roadblocks that today prevent us from going – even thinking – toward a desirable future. The necessary first step in such a defence, I have argued throughout this book, is defending serendipity against its false selves, i.e., against its illegitimate avatars that populate our current understanding of innovation and forward-looking practices in general. We have encountered many of these avatars in different shapes and forms throughout the chapters of this book: in the failed creative industries policies, in the changeless change gymnastics of 'social innovation', in the cynical practices of Digital Taylorism and the false hopes of mass-entrepreneurship, in the lunacy of techno-mysticism and singularity, in the sharing-fraud of platform capitalism, as well as in the hapless simulations of creative interdisciplinarity of contemporary HE.

What all these avatars share is an approach to serendipity that reduces it to a self-referential game where accidents might happen within the parameters set by the strict ideological limits of the present, that is to say, without the sagacity that is necessary for *kairos*, the arrow of time, to penetrate a future that positively differentiates itself from the present. The notion of serendipity has become part of the spiel of *Gegenwartseitelkeit*, or presentist vanity, thereby turning it into a weapon against itself, which is to say, a weapon against the future. To speak of a necessary defence of serendipity is thus anything but a call for semantic purity (how could we make such a call anyway, given its troubled etymology), but is instead an attempt to forge instruments that can help us overcome our present stasis.

So, the first thing we need to do is dispense with these simulations of serendipity, which also means to distance ourselves from the dominant ideologies of creativity and innovation. I am well aware that this is easier said than done, as many of us are existentially invested in these simulations and – despite increasing doubts and unease – are hard-pressed to call out their bluff. And yet, there simply is no way around admitting that the current approaches to 'making the world a better place' are failing, and often spectacularly so. Having said this, I still believe, as stated in the introduction, that serendipity can provide us with an important lead in our search for a way to a desirable future. As any serious analysis of our current practices of innovation makes clear, this can only work if we pull serendipity out from under the rubble of ideological simulation in order to rigorously relocate it at the level of society, of *Gesellschaft*. We need to apply serendipity to the social infrastructure that conditions our intellectual and material practice, both as citizens and professionals. Currently, this infrastructure is programmed in such a way as to prevent both thinking and practice towards a sustainable future. If I am not mistaken, then the above analysis allows us to identify two ideological culprits who carry at least some of the responsibility for our current bad programming: our unfaltering belief in the benevolent powers of digital technology and the illegitimate equation of innovation and entrepreneurship.[172]

172 The latter, I would like to add, is a particular articulation of a more comprehensive tendency, i.e., the illegitimate elevation of the market to the leading principle of social organisation precisely at a time when in the economy proper, it increasingly disappears. I have discussed this problem on several occasions throughout the book. See also: Thiel 2014.

With regard to digital technology, we have seen the paralysing effects of techno-mysticism on fields such as 'social innovation' and HE. What we have to understand in this respect is that – and I have said this repeatedly throughout the book – technology is a *pharmakon*, it can be both poison and cure with regard to the great challenges we are facing. Today, perhaps more than ever, we need a vision of what we want to achieve by way of technology. Which is, incidentally, the direct opposite of the infantile notion of technological singularity. And yet, even without wacky notions of digital redemption, the application of technology according to the logic of profit and/or social control bears a great amount of destructive potential. We have seen this with particular vividness in the chapters on Digital Taylorism and platform capitalism. There is enough evidence to disqualify those who argue that the Internet and digital technology provide us with an inbuilt mechanism that fosters the occurrence of serendipity by default. There is a potential, certainly, but it won't be realised unless the current bad programming is radically changed.

The question of the relation between entrepreneurship and innovation is slightly more difficult to address. Today, Schumpeter's notion that there is a strong connection between the two has mutated into the belief that turning everyone into an entrepreneur of oneself is the precondition for an innovative society. Again, I have addressed this throughout the book, but I would like to approach this question in a more fundamental way here by asking a seemingly naïve question: What is entrepreneurship in its essence? The French economist Frédéric Lordon tries to answer this question with reference to the Renaissance philosopher Benedict de Spinoza. Entrepreneurship, understood in its most general sense, is nothing but the desire to undertake (French: *entreprendre*, German: *unternehmen*, to undertake), to start something new. As such, it entertains a close relation to Spinoza's notion of *conatus*, designating "the thrust that changes the condition of something from rest to motion, the fundamental energy that shakes up the body and sets it on the course of pursuing some object".[173] In Spinoza's thought, *conatus* is the energy of life itself, the desire – indeed, the passion – from which we derive the will to go on, to go further, in order to creatively shape our existence. Entrepreneurship in this very fundamental sense is thus a specific expression of the vital passion that Spinoza calls *conatus*. Of course, Lordon says, entrepreneurship as expression of *conatus* needs to be historically situated, as the parameters of its possible articulation are set by the society in which it is able (or unable) to unfold:

> The history of each society is what both gives rise and sets limits to the range of undertakings [*entreprises*] that are possible within it, that is, to the range of objects of desires that a society considers legitimate. Free enterprise, in the most general sense of freedom to undertake – that is, in the sense of the conatus – is consequently nothing other than the freedom to desire and to set out in pursuit of one's desire.[174]

The promise to gain "the freedom to desire and to set out in pursuit of one's desire" is, of course, at the heart of the rhetoric that today promotes the idea of independent entrepreneurship. And because of this freedom to desire, our social innovators, creative professionals and independent entrepreneurs are expected to be the distributed yet systematic source and driver of innovation. Autonomous, full of great ideas, and super-connected, it is just a question of time before these masters of serendipity are struck by right kind of crowd or angel funding, push prototypes into serial production and scale brilliant inventions to great market success.

173   Lordon 2014: 2.
174   Ibid.

Yet, according to Spinoza, this may be so, but this does not mean at all that becoming entrepreneur would entail an increase in autonomous creativity or innovativeness. One needs to have, he would say, a fairly naïve understanding of subjectivity to believe such a thing. Spinoza, as we know, is a radical sceptic when it comes to the idea of an autonomous subject, claiming that "men are deceived in thinking themselves free, a belief that consists only in this, that they are conscious of their actions and ignorant of the causes by which they are determined." [175] According to Spinoza, the idea of an autonomous subject is totally illusory; intrinsic motivation, understood as action that emerges out of a free, self-determined interiority does simply not exist. In all our actions, we are radically heteronomous beings. And while in the 17th century, it needed an exceptional thinker like Spinoza to come to this conclusion, to us, who live in the age of the Internet, this is absolutely obvious and intuitive. We constantly move through clouds and networks whose interfaces never stop reminding us of this essential heteronomy. The Internet is a permanent Spinoza quote, visualising at every turn of our existence the extent to which we are entangled in a net of heteronomous influences. And yet, strangely, our contemporary cult of the heroic entrepreneur shows as well how much we are hanging on to this illusion.

It should be clear that contesting the notion of autonomy as self-determined, individual interiority does not mean that human agency is somehow remote-controlled. The power to act remains entirely ours but – and this is crucial – it is always already determined by an external field of prior forces. We have to give up our strong notion of individualism, but again, who could seriously hold on to that in a time when digital media constantly visualises our hetero-determination anyway? What we get in return is a more realistic notion of autonomy in terms of our power to

175   Spinoza 1996, II, 35, Scholium.

act as *direction*. In this sense, it is absolute nonsense to believe that setting out as entrepreneur would mean anything even close to becoming the sovereign over one's desire to act. One remains exogenously determined (owing everything to endless chains of external encounters), what changes is the architecture organising the external determination.

What this short detour through Spinozan thought reveals is that the effectiveness of innovation processes – be they techno-logical, economic, or, indeed, social in character – is not a function of the amount of smart minds that mingle in one room, one city, one region, etc. It is a function of how heterogeneously all these exogenously determined minds and bodies are able to think and 'make'. And right now, they are all thinking and making exactly the same. Hence, serendipity as an individual, psychological char-acteristic becomes utterly useless; the respective environments (hubs, coworking spaces, office designs, and so on) can be no more than absurd vanity fairs. Of course, this could change in the future – and so it should. However, what we need to understand is that without a social infrastructure that provides for heteroge-neity, dissent and real difference this is not going to happen. This is why I am convinced that we have to push our understanding of serendipity from the individual and its psyche to the level of society. We need more room: not to 'think outside the box' but to act outside the confines of the market (entrepreneurship) and the algorithmic logic of digital technology.

2. A Radical Politics of Innovation

The much more challenging question, of course, is how to get there, how to reach a situation in which a social infrastructure programmed for the sake of a more serendipitous, that is, neces-sarily, a more participative, democratic and equal society becomes even a possibility. *Deconstructing* the myths of individualistic heroism, technological redemption, and so on is an absolutely necessary first step, but no more than that. It needs to be accompanied by a much more *constructive* movement, one that creates shared visions of a desirable future. Of course, we can and should go on using reason to debunk the errors and quasi-religious beliefs that in the name of creativity, innovation and, indeed, serendipity do nothing but prolong our current stasis. In fact, I hope this book provides a modest contribution to efforts of this kind. However, this kind of reasoning and critique is not, in our world, sufficient if we want to change this situation substantially. What an effective reopening toward the future requires is an effort to conceive and construct a politics that is *radical* in so far as it goes to the root of our current innovation predicament. It should be obvious that these final pages cannot provide a blueprint for such a radical politics of innovation. However, a question that can and should be addressed here is that of the *place* where this radical political effort should be located in order to generate the innovation we feel is needed today. What does it mean, then, to say that serendipity has to be addressed at the level of society? Where, exactly, do we have to locate the level of politics with regard to radical innovation?

In a widely noted discussion with Yanis Varoufakis and Slavoj Žižek in London in late November 2015, Wikileaks founder Julian Assange made a statement that is highly interesting in the present context. There are today, Assange said, only two ideologies operating with great effectiveness on the world stage: radical Islam and Silicon Valley's high-tech liberalism. What he meant by this, he explained, was that only those two belief-systems are powerful enough to mobilise large populations for the purpose of changing the world. To avoid misunderstandings, Assange did not intend to equate the worldview of the digital oligarchs and their following with the despicable terrorist extremism that, in the name of God, aims at the enslavement of humanity according to a reductive perversion of the rules of Islam. What he was trying to express is his concern about the fact that the two belief-systems most powerful today when it comes to the mobilisation of 'hearts and minds' are ideologies that – albeit in very different ways – reject and actively work against the achievements of emancipatory politics and enlightenment values. This should be obvious for the case of radical Islam, but it is equally true for Silicon Valley's war against democracy and the values of enlightenment that has been the object of analysis throughout this book.[176]

What is surprising about Assange's statement is that it comes from someone who was, and, despite his confinement, still is, part of a network of communities and groups that are inspired by a much more democratic and participative worldview. The Wikileaks group may be somewhat more radical than some of its peers, but by and large it belongs to the distributed movement of innumerable hackers, activists, innovators, social designers, transition towners, impact makers for good causes, sustainability activists and so on whose minds are set on making the world a better place. And yet, even with the knowledge of Wikileaks' own impact – expressed most vividly by his factual incarceration – Assange believes that their worldview is no match for either of the two dominant ideologies.

Unfortunately, Assange's assessment is much more realist than it is defeatist. The realism of his analysis has nothing to do with the lack of appeal of democracy and equality or any such thing. Again, there are, in Europe alone, tens or maybe hundreds of thousands of (often young) people working day in, day out on projects inspired by worldviews that might be different in certain aspects but converge on positive values that continue in modern form the European tradition of the Enlightenment. The reason why these distributed communities of activists remain toothless

---

176 For those who remain unconvinced I suggest a close reading of Eric Schmidt's own manifesto *How Google Works* (Schmidt & Rosenberg 2014).

and politically ineffective is precisely that they are *distributed communities*. They have given up on the idea of politics as the process by which an ideology peacefully conquers the modern centre of power, i.e., the state. Just like the hippies in the 1960s, they see the state as a corrupt, bureaucratic machine that today is in the hands of an opportunistic managerial class whose only value seems to be the preservation of their own power. Yet, as I have argued in Chapter 2, the fact that the state does not function effectively as an agent of desirable change does not mean that it can simply be bypassed. It remains the greatest centre of power even though there is no denying that neoliberal politics has weakened it *vis-à-vis* the powers of economic and financial rationality.

Of course, one cannot but have the greatest sympathies for those who are arguing that "in small groups and communities we can at least do something", "small steps are better than no steps", "better to do something in your local context than do nothing at all", and so on. The reason why these efforts don't acquire political efficacy is that in order to partake in the social resources they need for survival they have to align with (or, at the very least, not contradict) the objectives of the bad programming that is neoliberal politics. The situation is analogous to that of the entrepreneurs discussed in Chapter 7: the bottleneck of the market that prevents economic innovation is reproduced here as the bottleneck of social innovation. The only way to pass through it is by conforming to the standards of political stasis. Hence, the greatest political challenge today is to break this bottleneck in order to unleash society's powers of invention and innovation. And this means to liberate the state from its current bad programming done by the misdirected hackers of neoliberal politics.

Abandoning the state for the more intimate politics of community is a strategy that plays in the hands of those who profit from the current stasis of our societies. What we have to realise – and urgently so – is that the state is not in its essence the closed managerial monolith we are seeing today but a potentially flexible hardware in dire need of better programming. The issue here is not an unreflective return to the politics of the state, but the recognition that dealing with the state cannot be avoided. The reason why the neoliberal state euphorically embraces the 'change makers' is exactly their ignorance with regard to the reality of political power relations. It has allowed the neoliberal state to construct a pseudo-counterculture in its own image that it uses like a smart firewall against any real disruption of its current programming. If we want to create the conditions for a serendipitous society that finds its expression in a social infrastructure of equality and participation, we have to confront real existing power relations instead of dreamily looking the other, i.e. communal, way. In other words, we have to confront the state as well. In this respect, it might be worthwhile to go back to the German sociologist Helmuth Plessner, who, nearly a hundred years ago, expressed a vision of the state as an open system mediating between the spheres of community [*Gemeinschaft*] and society [*Gesellschaft*]:

> The state is a procedure and not a substance; it is an open system of measures that elevate the demands of the public sphere out of their unforeseeability and indeterminacy and to align the communal need of each person to his natural right for warmth and trust and to prevent the danger of continual friction and interference between the two spheres. The state is the systematisation of the public sphere in the service of community and the epitome of measures protecting the community in the service of the public sphere.[177]

It is fascinating how Plessner's observations, intended as a measured defence of the bourgeois, democratic state against attacks from left and right radicals, ring themselves quite radical to the

177 Plessner 2001: 115.

contemporary ear, trained as it is in decades of neoliberal rhetoric. Of course, what Plessner has to say remains incredibly instructive today precisely because it clarifies the irreducible relationship between community and the state in the notion of the public sphere. And it is exactly in the mutilation of the public sphere that the detrimental effects of neoliberal politics can be most clearly observed. The problem is that the neoliberal hatred for the public sphere finds its unintended support network in the communities of activists and 'change makers' and their rejection of 'traditional' politics. In their view, the state has failed as a model for bringing about social change. They are convinced that the multitude of communities working alongside each other, designing, hacking and urban gardening for the social good, will reach in the near future a point of critical mass out of which a new and more desirable society will be born. Just like Ferdinand Tönnies at the end of the 19th century, they believe that community represents a more authentic form of sociability; one that is ontologically prior to society and therefore the ideal locus from which a new society can and should be created. For them, community articulates the principle of 'the commons' – that which belongs to all and therefore to nobody in particular – as the sacred foundation of society. Today's proliferation of communal care for the commons, supported not least by the democratising powers of the Internet, is taken to be the unmistakable sign of an approaching moment in socio-evolution, the arrival of which is going to lead to the realisation of the commons on a grand scale.[178]

What makes this kind of thinking politically useless is that it is, in its essence, magical. It understands the development of human society as a teleological process, at the end of which there will be an ontological revolution in the very sense of the word: that which

178   E.g. Eisenstein 2011. Variations of this argument can also be found throughout the work of the Italian Post-Autonomists from Negri to Agamben.

is just and good in society but right now exists only as its hidden foundation will rise to the surface, burying the excrescences of power and injustice underneath the rubble of history. It reproduces the magical logic of technological singularity discussed in Chapter 4, wrapped in an utterly ahistorical understanding of social and political processes, sacrificing any notion of politics to a quasi-religious belief in socio-ontological redemption. It is in this sense that the focus on community-based approaches for the renewal of our societies is not only futile but also dangerous: it justifies a pseudo-substitute for agonistic politics that deflects from the real challenge of creating the conditions for a society able to serendipitously move into a desirable future. Richard Sennett analysed this tendency in the 1970s, and his diagnosis has never been more topical:

> Community becomes a weapon against society, whose great vice is now seen to be its impersonality. But a community of power can only be an illusion in a society like that of the industrial West, one in which stability has been achieved by a progressive extension to the international scale of structures of economic control. In sum, the belief in direct human relations on an intimate scale has seduced us from converting our understanding of the realities of power into guides for our political behavior. The result is that the forces of domination or inequity remain unchallenged.[179]

Again, a wide variety of community-based inspiration is absolutely crucial when it comes to imagining a more desirable future society, but as a political instrument, community is absolutely useless. Yes, community represents a more authentic and, indeed, organic expression of sociability, but it is exactly this characteristic that

179   Sennett 1977: 339.

activism needs to shed in order to become politically efficacious. The name of this political efficacy – as Plessner, Sennett and many others have taught us – is the public sphere. The public sphere is by definition *abstract*, but it is its abstractness that defines its political value. It is abstract in the sense that its very existence can only be ensured by a permanent creative struggle, transcending individual and community for the sake of their future existence. As a social abstraction, it requires the labour of politics, for which the community, due to its organic, concrete nature, has no need. Only through the labour of politics can the public sphere be actualised and community acquire political meaning. Yet, in spite of its abstraction, the public sphere is anything but a 'heartless' place. As Bernard Stiegler reminds us, politics as the perpetual reinvention of the public sphere thrives on the investment of *philia* (affection) and sym-pathy in the creative affirmation of a form of sociability that transcends the authentic narrowness of community.[180] The public sphere is where communal *philia* and sym-pathy are transformed into the care for the social infrastructure that conditions the existence (or inexistence) of what we call society. The paradox that modern, complex societies have to endure is that such *collective caring* is always and necessarily a *polemical* process (from the Greek word for war: *polemos*). It needs conflict and dissent in the encounter of communal and individual difference in order to remain open to its possible futures. And this is exactly the reason why the public sphere is the logical habitat of serendipity as a force for social good. Today, a radical politics of innovation must be directed toward the recapture of the state by an ideology that is a polemic for the reinvention of a public sphere whose accidental sagacity will generate potential futures we don't even dare to dream about.

180   Stiegler 2014a: Chapter 1.

Acknowledgments

My interest in serendipity originated in the early Noughties, when I grappled with the then emerging creative industries discourse. I was particularly fascinated with the use of the notion of serendipity by those entrepreneurial activists who were trying to create (coworking and similar) spaces that they hoped would defy the traditional logic of economic practice. For a while I thought that these experiments had the potential of growing into a broad movement, mobilising within the precariat the kind of solidarity and indeed, serendipity necessary to counter the hyper-exploitative tendencies of neoliberal capitalism. In hindsight, it is clear that my early enthusiasm was rather overoptimistic. However, being part of the consulting-driven world of creative industries, innovation and all the rest of it, gave me invaluable insights into the practical workings of neoliberal ideology. In fact, I am rather grateful for this experience, as it motivated me to write this book, whose analysis, I hope, profited from it as well. And yet, what has happened to me over the course of the past fifteen or so years I increasingly see happening all around me. One can literally feel the disenchantment and frustration among all those who time and again join changeless change projects in the hope that this time it's not going to be mere ideological therapy but the real deal – which, of course, it never is. We have come to a point where it takes quite a bit of cynicism to keep up even the appearance of enthusiasm for the dominant simulations of creativity and innovation. If there is anything that I would like for this book to achieve then it is to show that one can speak out against this nonsense and actually do so *in the name of innovation*. This, I believe, is the kind of disruption we need today, because innovation for the sake of a desirable future is simply too important to leave to the profiteers of the current neoliberal stasis and their willing ideological accomplices.

The actual writing process for *In Defence of Serendipity* began in early 2014, when Geert Lovink offered me a one-year research grant at his Institute of Network Cultures in Amsterdam. Geert has been a great intellectual companion in the journey that led to this publication and an invaluable source of motivation as well. Without him, I doubt this book would have seen the light of day. Mark Fisher was as kind as to take the gamble to commission this book. I am grateful for his comments and encouragement that helped me through those moments of doubt known to every writer. Many thanks also to the team at Repeater Books, in particular to Tariq Goddard, who is everything one could wish for in a publisher.

I am indebted to many friends and colleagues who helped me improve earlier versions of this manuscript. My greatest debt here is to Geert Lovink and Hartmut Wilkening, on whom I could always rely as meticulous first readers and rigorous critics. Individual chapters and parts of the manuscript profited from the critical attention of brilliant minds such as Justin O'Connor, Sarah Sharma, Matthias Weber, Söhnke Zehle, Claudia Brückner, Holm Friebe, Philipp Albers, Ned Rossiter and Roberta Comunian. Special thanks go to Brian Holmes who generously shared his insights into the history of Silicon Valley.

Yet, those I owe by far the most for the completion of this book are my wife Sandra Trienekens and my son Karl. Sandra's intellectual companionship is one of the great gifts of my life; our conversations and (at times rather fierce) arguments have helped shape my thinking on many of the issues discussed in this book. And seeing Karl grow up reminds me every day of the importance of intellectual integrity and rigour when it comes to thinking about the future, as it is a crucial part of taking care of the younger generations. Both of them have been incredibly supportive, particularly during the last months of writing, when I tested their patience with long hours of absence, sitting in my studio in Amsterdam, working away on this book. I cannot, of course, give back those nights and weekends, but the least I can do is dedicate this book to them.

Literature

Alliez, Eric (2004) 'The Difference and Repetition of Gabriel Tarde', *Distinktion*, 9, pp. 49-54.

— (1999) 'Tarde et le Probleme de la Constitution', in: Tarde, Gabriel, *Monadologie et Sociologie*, Paris: Institut Synthélabo, pp. 9-32.

Anderson, Chris (2006) *The Long Tail: Why the Future of Business is Selling Less of More*, New York: Hyperion.

Anker, Peder (2010) *From Bauhaus to Ecohouse: A History of Ecological Design*, Baton Rouge: Louisiana State University Press.

Aristotle (1941) 'Nichomachean Ethics', in Richard McKeon (ed.), *The Basic Works of Aristotle*, New York: Random House.

Armbrüster, Thomas & Kipping, Matthias (2002-3) 'Strategy Consulting at the Crossroads', *International Studies of Management & Organization*, 32 (4), pp. 19-42.

Arthur, Charles (2014) 'UK orders "Sharing Economy" Review - But Workers Need Not Apply', *The Guardian*, Sept. 29th, http://www. theguardian.com/technology/2014/sep/29/uk-government-or- ders-sharing-economy-review-but-workers-need-not-apply.

Aschoff, Nicole (2015) *The New Prophets of Capital*, London: Verso.

Barbrook, Richard (2007) *Imaginary Futures: From Thinking Machines to the Global Village*, London: Pluto Press.

Barbrook, Richard & Cameron, Andy (1995) 'The Californian Ideology', *MUTE* 3(1), http://www.metamute.org/editorial/articles/califor- nian-ideology#.

Baudrillard, Jean (1975) *The Mirror of Production*, St. Louis: Telos.

Bauman, Zygmunt (2006) *Liquid Fear*, Cambridge: Polity.

— (2003) *Liquid Love: On the Frailty of Human Bonds*, Cambridge: Polity.

— (2000) *Liquid Modernity*, Cambridge: Polity

— (1989) *Modernity and The Holocaust*, Ithaca, N.Y.: Cornell University Press.

Berardi, Franco (2011) *After the Future*, tr. Adrianna Bove, Melinda Cooper, Erik Empson, Enrico, Giuseppina Mecchia & Tiziana Terranova, ed. Gary Genosko & Nicholas Thoburn, Edinburgh: AK Press.

Black, Liam (2013) 'The Poor Are Not the Raw Material for Your Salvation', *Pioneers Post*, April 10, https://www.pioneerspost.com/comment/20130410/letter-young-social-entrepreneur-the-poor-are-not-the-raw-material-your-salvation.

Blume, Eugen; Feli, Matilda; Knapstein, Gabriele & Nichols, Catherine (2015) *Black Mountain: An Interdisciplinary Experiment 1933 -1957*, Leipzig: Spector Books.

Boltanski, Luc & Chappello, Eve (2006) *Le Nouvel Esprit du Capitalisme*, Paris: Gallimard.

Botsman, Rachel & Rogers Roo (2010) *What's Mine Is Yours: The Rise of Collaborative Consumption*, New York: Harper Collins.

Bowker, Geof (1993) 'How to Be Universal: Some Cybernetic Strategies, 1943-70', *Social Studies of Science*, 23 (1), pp. 107-127.

Braudel, Fernand (1992) *Civilization and Capitalism, 15th-18th Century, Vol. III: The Perspective of the World*, trans. Sian Reynold, Oakland, CA: University of California Press.

Bria, Francesca (2015) *Growing a Digital Social Innovation Ecosystem for Europe*, http://www.nesta.org.uk/publications/growing-digital-social-innovation-ecosystem-europe#sthash.sJiUFHYs.dpuf.

Brown, Eliot (2015) 'WeWork's Valuation Soars to $10 Billion', *The Wall Street Journal*, June 24, http://www.wsj.com/articles/valuation-of-shared-office-provider-wework-soars-to-10-billion-1435181485.

Brynjolfsson, Erik & McAfee, Andrew (2014) *The Second Machine Age: Work, Progress, and Prosperity in a Time of Brilliant Technologies*, New York: Norton & Company.

Burroughs, William S. (1970) *The Electronic Revolution*, Göttingen: Expanded Media Editions.

Carr, Nicholas (2010) *The Shallows: What the Internet Is Doing to Our Brains*, New York: Noton & Company.

Christensen, Clayton M. & Van Bever, Derek (2014) 'The Capitalist's Dilemma', *Harvard Business Review*, June, https://hbr.org/2014/06/the-capitalists-dilemma.

Caygill, Howard (2013) *On Resistance: A Philosophy of Defiance*, London: Bloomsbury.

Cnossen, Boukje & Olma, Sebastian (2014) *The Volkskrant Building: Manufacturing Difference in Amsterdam's Creative City*, Amsterdam: Amsterdam Creative Industries Publishing.

Cohen-Cole, Jamie (2014) *The Open Mind: Cold War Politics and the Sciences of Human Nature,* University of Chicago Press.

Collini, Stefan (2012) *What Are Universities For?*, London: Penguin Books.

Conway, Flo & Siegelman, Jim (2006) *Dark Hero of the Information Age: In Search of Norbert Wiener The Father of Cybernetics*, New York: Basic Books.

Cox, Andrew & Lonsdale, Chris (1997) 'Strategic Outsourcing Methodologies in UK Companies', *CBSP Working Paper*, Birmingham: University of Birmingham.

Dao, Francisco (2013) 'Haves and Have Nots in the Sharing Economy', *Pando*, 7 May, https://pando.com/2013/05/07/haves-and-have-nots-in-the-sharing-economy .

Davenport, Thomas H. & Short, James E. (1990) 'The New Industrial Engineering: Information Technology and Business Process Redesign', *Sloan Management Review*, 31 (4), pp. 11-26.

Davies, William (2015) *The Happiness Industry. How the Government and Big Business Sold Us Well-Being*, London: Verso.

Davis, Erik (1998) *TechGnosis: Myth, Magic, and Mysticism in the Age of Information*, New York: Harmony Books.

DCMS (Department of Culture, Media and Sport) (1998/2001), *Creative Industry Task Force: Mapping Document*, London.

Debord, Guy (1994) *The Society of the Spectacle*, trans. D. Nicholson-Smith, New York: Zone Books.

Deleuze, Gilles (1995) 'Postscript on Control Societies', in: *Negotiations 1972-1990*, trans. Martin Joughin, New York: Columbia University Press, pp. 177-182.

Deleuze, Gilles & Guattari, Félix (1994) *What Is Philosophy?* trans. Hugh Tomlinson and Graham Burchill, London: Verso.

Dery, Mark (1996) *Escape Velocity: Cyberculture at the End of the Century*, New York: Grove Press.

Dick, Philip K. (1981) *VALIS*, London: Orion Books.

Diederichsen, Diedrich (2010) 'Kreative Arbeit und Selbstverwirklichung', in: Menke, Christoph & Rebentisch, Juliane (eds.) *Kreation und Depression. Freiheit im Gegenwärtigen Kapitalismus*, Berlin: Kadmos, pp. 118-128.

Durkheim, Émile (1982) *The Rules of Sociological Method*, edited with an introduction by Steven Lukes, trans. W.D. Halls, New York: The Free Press.

Dwyer, Paula (2015) 'Rubio's Old Ideas for New Gig Economy', *Bloomber-View*, 8 October, http://www.bloombergview.com/articles/2015-10-08/rubio-s-ideas-for-young-gig-economy-just-sound-old.

Eisenstein, Charles (2011) *Sacred Economics: Money, Gift, and Society in the Age of Transition*, Berkeley, Ca.: Evolver.

Elliott, Larry & Atkinson, Dan (2007) *Fantasy Island. Waking Up To The Incredible Economic, Political & Social Illusions Of The Blair Legacy*, London: Constable.

Eskow, Richard (2015) 'The Sharing Economy Is a Lie: Uber, Ayn Rand and the Truth about Tech and Libertarians', *Salon*, 1 February, http://www.salon.com/2015/02/01/the_sharing_economy_is_a_lie_uber_ayn_rand_and_the_truth_about_tech_and_libertarians/.

Fisher, Mark (2009) *Capitalist Realism: Is There No Alternative?*, London: Zero Books.

Foucault, Michel (2008) *The Birth of Biopolitics: Lectures at the Collège de France, 1978-1979*, trans. Graham Burchell, Basingstoke: Palgrave-Macmillan.

Franke, Answelm & Diederichsen, Diedrich (ed.) (2013) *The Whole Earth. California and the Disappearance of the Outside*, Berlin: Sternberg Press.

Friebe, Holm (2014) *Die Steinstrategie: Von der Kunst, Nicht zu Handeln*, München: Hanser.

Friebe, Holm & Lobo, Sascha (2006) *Wir nennen es Arbeit: Die Digitale Bohème oder: Intelligentes Leben jenseits der Festanstellung*, München: Heyne.

Galison, Peter (1999) 'Trading Zone. Coordinating Action and Belief', in Mario Biagioli (ed.) *The Science Studies Reader*, London: Routledge, pp. 137-159.

— (1994) 'The Ontology of the Enemy: Norbert Wiener and the Cybernetic Vision', *Critical Inquiry* 21(1), pp. 228-266.

Gallup, Inc. (2013) *The State of the Global Workplace: Employee Engagement Insights for Business Leaders Worldwide*, http://www.gallup.com/services/178517/state-global-workplace.aspx.

Gibbs, Samuel (2015) 'Musk, Wozniak and Hawking Urge Ban on Warfare AI and Autonomous Weapons', *The Guardian*, 27 July, http://www.theguardian.com/technology/2015/jul/27/musk-wozniak-hawking-ban-ai-autonomous-weapons.

Gill, Rosalind & Pratt, Andy (2008) 'In the Social Factory? Immaterial Labour, Precariousness and Cultural Work', *Theory, Culture & Society.* 25 (7-8), pp. 1-30.

Graeber, David (2015) *The Utopia of Rules: On Technology, Stupidity, and the Secret Joys of Bureaucracy*, New York: Melville House.

— (2013) 'On the Phenomenon of Bullshit Jobs', *Strike! Magazine*, http://strikemag.org/bullshit-jobs/.

Greenblatt, Stephen (2011) *The Swerve: How the World Became Modern*, New York: Norton & Company.

Hagel, John; Seely Brown, John; Davison, Lang (2010) *The Power of Pull: How Small Moves, Smartly Made, Can Set Big Things in Motion*, New York: Basic Books.

Hammer, Michael & Champy, James (1993) *Reengineering the Corporation: A Manifesto for Business Revolution*, New York: Harper Business.

Han, Byung-Chul (2015) *The Burnout Society*, Stanford: Stanford University Press.

— (2014) *Psychopolitik. Neoliberalismus und die Neuen Machttechniken*, Frankfurt am Main: Fischer.

— (2010) *Müdigkeitsgesellschaft*, Berlin: Matthes & Seitz.

Hardt, Michael and Negri, Antonio (2000) *Empire*, Cambridge, Mass.: Harvard University Press.

Harris, Catherine L. (1987) 'Office Automation: Making it All Pay Off', *Business Week*, October 12, pp. 134-146.

Hatherley, Owen (2010) *A Guide to the New Ruins of Great Britain*, London: Verso.

Hayles, Katherine (1999) *How We Became Posthuman. Virtual Bodies in Cybernetics, Literature and Informatics*, Chicago: Chicago University Press.

Head, Simon (2014) *Mindless: Why Smarter Machines are Making Dumber Humans*, New York: Basic Books.

— (2005) *The New Ruthless Economy: Work and Power in the Digital Age*, Oxford: Oxford University Press.

Hellas, Paul & Morris, Paul (1992) *Values of the Enterprise Culture: The Moral Debate*, London: Routledge.

Heartfield, James (2005) *The Creativity Gap*, http://www.design4design.com/broadsides/creative.pdf.

Hochschild, Arlie R. (1985) *The Managed Heart. Commercialization of Human Feeling*, Berkeley: University of California Press.

Hörl, Erich (2008) 'Das kybernetischen Bild des Denkens', in: Hagner, Michael & Hörl, Erich (eds.) *Die Transformation des Humanen. Beiträge zur Kulturgeschichte der Kybernetik*, Frankfurt am Main: Suhrkamp.

Holmes, Brian (2009) 'Future Map, or, How the Cyborgs Learned to Stop Worrying and Love Surveillance', in *Escape the Overcode. Activist Art in the Control Society*, Eindhoven: Van Abbemuseum, pp. 304-327.

Howaldt, Jürgen, Kopp, Ralf & Schwarz, Michael (2013) *Zur Theorie sozialer Innovationen: Tardes vernachlässigter Beitrag zur Entwicklung einer soziologischen Innovationstheorie*, Weinheim: Beltz-Juventa.

Howkins, John (2009) *Creative Ecologies: Where Thinking Is a Proper Job*, London: Penguin.

Isaacson, Walter (2014) *The Innovators: How a Group of Hackers, Geniuses, and Geeks Created the Digital Revolution*, New York: Simon & Schuster.

ITRS (2015) *International Technology Roadmap for Semiconductors 2.0*, http://www.semiconductors.org/main/2015_international_technology_roadmap_for_semiconductors_itrs/.

Johnson, Steven (2010) *Where Good Ideas Come From: The Natural History of Innovation*, New York: Penguin Books.

Johns, Tammy & Gratton, Linda (2013) "The Third Wave Of Virtual Work," *Harvard Business Review*, 91(1/2), pp. 66 - 73.

Kaminska, Izabella (2015) 'The Sharing Economy Will Go Medieval on You', *Financial Times*, May 21: http://ftalphaville.ft.com/2015/05/21/2130111/the-sharing-economy-will-go-medieval-on-you/.

Kanter, Rosabeth Moss (2015) *Move: Putting America's Infrastructure Back in the Lead*, New York: Norton & Company.

Kaufman, Micha (2014) 'Trust Each Other, The Sharing Economy Is Here to Stay', *Forbes*, 16 May, http://www.forbes.com/sites/michakaufman/2014/05/16/sharingeconomy/.

Keen, Andrew (2015) *The Internet is not the Answer*, London: Atlantic Books.

Kessler, Andy (2014) 'Brian Chesky: The "Sharing Economy" and Its Enemies', *The Wall Street Journal*, Jan. 17: http://www.wsj.com/news/articles/SB10001424052702304049704579321001856708992.

Kessler, Sarah (2015) 'The Sharing Economy Is Dead, And We Killed It', *Fast Company*, Sept. 15: http://www.fastcompany.com/3050775/the-sharing-economy-is-dead-and-we-killed-it.

Kingdon, Matt (2012) *The Science of Serendipity: How to Unlock the Promise of Innovation*, Chichester: Wiley & Sons.

Kipping, Matthias (2002) 'Trapped in Their Wave: The Evolution of Management Consultancies', in Timothy Clark and Robin Fincham (eds.), *Critical Consulting: New Perspectives on the Management Advice Industry*, Malden, Mass.: Blackwell Publishers, pp. 28-49.

Kurzweil, Ray (2005) *The Singularity Is Near: When Humans Transcend Biology*, New York: Viking.

— (1999) *The Age of Spiritual Machines*, New York: Viking Penguin.

Lacy, Sarah (2015) 'The Truth about Uber in China', *Pando*, 31 August, https://pando.com/2015/08/31/truth-about-uber-china/.

Landry, Charles (1995) *The Creative City: A Toolkit for Urban Innovators* London: Routledge.

Latour, Bruno (2002) 'Gabriel Tarde and the End of the Social', in Patrick Joyce (ed.), *The Social in Question: New Bearings in History and the Social Sciences*, London: Routledge, pp. 117-132.

Lazzarato, Maurizio (2002) *Puissances de l'Invention: La Psychologie Économique de Gabriel Tarde contre l'Économie Politique*, Paris: Les Empêcheurs de Penser en Rond.

Leadbeater, Charles (2015) 'The Whirlpool Economy', *Nesta*, 12 March, http://www.nesta.org.uk/blog/whirlpool-economy.

Lee, Martin A. & Shlain, Bruce (1985) *Acid Dreams: The Complete Social History of LSD: The CIA, the Sixties, and Beyond*, New York: Grove Press.

Licklider, Joseph Carl Robnett (1963) *Topics for Discussion at the Forthcoming Meeting, Memorandum For: Members and Affiliates of the Intergalactic Computer Network*, Washington, D.C.: Advanced Research Projects Agency, *via KurzweilAI.net*, retrieved 14-09-2015.

— (1960) 'Man-Computer Symbiosis', *IRE Transactions on Human Factors in Electronics*, March, pp. 4-11.

Lobo, Sascha (2014) 'Die Mensch-Maschine: Auf dem Weg in die Dumping-hölle', *Spiegel Online*, 3 September, http://www.spiegel.de/netzwelt/netzpolitik/sascha-lobo-sharing-economy-wie-bei-uber-ist-plattform-kapitalismus-a-989584.html.

Lordon, Frédéric (2014) *Willing Slaves of Capital. Spinoza & Marx on Desire*, London: Verso.

Lorey, Isabell (2015) *State of Insecurity. Government of the Precarious*, London: Verso.

Lotringer, Silvère & Virilio, Paul (2005) *The Accident of Art*, New York: Semiotext(e).

Lovink, Geert & Rossiter, Ned (2007) *MyCreativity Reader: Critique of Creative Industries*, Amsterdam: Institute of Network Cultures.

Lucretius (2001) *De Rerum Natura: On the Nature of Things*, trans. with introduction and notes by Martin Ferguson Smith, Indianapolis: Hackett Publishing.

Marshall, Colin (2014) 'Downtown and Out? The Truth about Tony Hsieh's $350m Las Vegas Project', *The Guardian*, November 20, http://www.theguardian.com/cities/2014/nov/20/downtown-and-out-the-truth-about-tony-hsiehs-350m-las-vegas-project.

Martin, Roger L. & Osberg, Sally (2007) 'Social Entrepreneurship: The Case for Definition', *Stanford Social Innovation Review*, Spring, http://ssir.org/articles/entry/social_entrepreneurship_the_case_for_definition.

Mazzucato, Marina (2013) *The Entrepreneurial State: Debunking Public vs. Private Sector Myths*, London: Anthem Press.

McCulloch, Warren S. & Pitts, Walter H. (1943) 'A Logical Calculus of the Ideas Immanent in Nervous Activity', *Bulletin of Mathematical Biophysics*, (5), pp. 115-133.

McKenna, Christopher D. (2006) *The World's Newest Profession: Management Consulting in the Twentieth Century*, Cambridge, Mass.: Cambridge University Press.

McLuhan, Marshall (1964) *Understanding Media: The Extensions of Man*, London: Routledge & Kegan Paul.

— (1962) *Gutenberg Galaxy: The Making of Typographic Man*, Toronto: University of Toronto Press.

Merton, Robert & Barber Eleanor (2004) *The Travels and Adventures of Serendipity: A Study in Sociological Semantics and the Sociology of Science*. Princeton: Princeton University Press.

Mills, C.Wright (2000) *The Sociological Imagination*, 40th Anniversary Edition, Oxford: Oxford University Press.

Mims, Christopher (2015) 'How Everyone Gets the "Sharing" Economy Wrong', *The Wall Street Journal*, May 15: http://www.wsj.com/articles/how-everyone-gets-the-sharing-economy-wrong-1432495921.

Mirowski, Philip (2002) *Machine Dreams: Economics Becomes a Cyborg Science*, Cambridge: Cambridge University Press.

Möntmann, Nina (ed.) (2014) *Brave New Work – Schöne Neue Arbeit*, Hamburg: Walther König.

Morozov, Evgeny (2014) 'Don't Believe the Hype, the "Sharing Economy" Masks a Failing Economy', *The Guardian*, Sept. 28: http://www.theguardian.com/commentisfree/2014/sep/28/sharing-economy-internet-hype-benefits-overstated-evgeny-morozov.

— (2013a) *To Save Everything, Click Here: Technology, Solutionism, and the Urge to Fix Problems that Don't Exist*, New York: Allen Lane.

— (2013b) 'The Meme Hustler. Tim O'Reilly's Crazy Talk', *The Baffler*, No. 22: http://thebaffler.com/salvos/the-meme-hustler.

Muller, Thor & Becker, Lane (2012) *Get Lucky: How to Put Planned Serendipity to Work for You and Your Business*, San Francisco: Jossey-Bass.

Mulgan, Geoff (2013) *Setting a Future Research Agenda for Social Innovation*, Keynote Speech at the Social Frontiers Conference, GCU, London, 14th November, https://www.youtube.com/watch?v=dER0EFOVQ50.

Mumford, Lewis (1970) *The Myth of the Machine, Vol. 2: The Pentagon of Power*, New York: Harcourt Brace Jovanovich Publishers.

Mumford, Lewis (1967) *The Myth of the Machine, Vol.1: Technics and Human Development* New York: Harcourt Brace Jovanovich Publishers.

Murray, Robin; Caulier-Grice, Julie & Mulgan, Geoff (2010) *The Open Book of Social Innovation*. London: NESTA, http://www.nesta.org.uk/sites/default/files/the_open_book_of_social_innovation.pdf.

Negri, Antonio (1991) *The Savage Anomaly: The Power of Spinoza's Metaphysics and Politics*, trans. Michael Hardt, Minneapolis: University of Minnesota Press.

Oakley, Kate & O'Connor, Justin (2015) *The Routledge Companion to the Cultural Industries*, London: Routledge.

O'Neill, William L. (1971) *Coming Apart: An Informal History of America in the 1960s*, ChicagoL Ivan R. Dee Publisher.

Osborne, David & Gaebler, Ted (1992) *Reinventing Government: How the Entrepreneurial Spirit Is Transforming the Public Sector*, Reading, MA.: Addison-Wesley.

Peck, Jamie (2005) 'Struggling with the Creative Class', *International Journal of Urban and Regional Research*, 29 (4), pp. 740-770.

Peters, Tom (1999) *The Brand You 50: Or: Fifty Ways to Transform Yourself from an "Employee" into a Brand That Shouts Distinction, Commitment, and Passion!*, New York: Knopf/Random House.

Peukert, Detlef J. K. (1989) *Max Webers Diagnose der Moderne*, Göttingen: Vandenhoeck und Ruprecht.

Piketty, Thomas (2014) *Capital in the Twenty-First Century*, trans. Arthur Goldhammer, Cambridge, Mass.: Harvard University Press.

Pine, B. Joseph, and Gilmore, James H. (1999) *The Experience Economy*, Boston: Harvard Business Press.

Plato (2009) *Protagoras*, trans. C.C.W. Taylor, Oxford: Oxford University Press."

Plessner, Helmuth (2001) *Die Grenzen der Gemeinschaft. Eine Kritik des Sozialen Radikalismus*, Frankfurt am Main: Suhrkamp.

Pol, Eduardo & Ville, Simon (2009) "Social innovation: Buzz word or enduring term?", *The Journal of Socio-Economics*, 38(6), pp. 878-885.

PricewaterhouseCoopers (2015) 'The Sharing Economy', *Consumer Intelligence Service*, April, http://www.pwc.com/us/en/industry/entertainment-media/publications/consumer-intelligence-series/sharing-economy.html.

Priddat, Birger (2002) 'Das Verschwinden der Langen Verträge', in Dirk Baecker (ed.), *Archäologie der Arbeit*, Berlin: Kulturverl. Kadmos, pp. 65-86.

Prigogine, Ilya & Stengers, Isabelle (1984) Order out of Chaos, University of Michigan: Bantam Books.

Raunig, Gerald; Ray, Gene & Wuggenig, Ulf (eds.) (2011) Critique of Creativity: *Precarity, Subjectivity and Resistance in the 'Creative Industries'*, London: MayFlyBooks.

Reckwitz , Andreas (1995) *Die Erfindung der Kreativität - Zum Prozess gesellschaftlicher Ästhetisierung*, Frankfurt: Surhkamp.

Rifkin, Jeremy (2014) *The Zero Marginal Cost Society: The Internet of Things, the Collaborative Commons, and the Eclipse of Capitalism*, New York: Palgrave Macmillan.

— (2011) *The Third Industrial Revolution: How Lateral Power Is Transforming Energy, the Economy, and the World*, New York: Palgrave Macmillan.

— (2009) *The Empathic Civilization: The Race to Global Consciousness in a World in Crisis*, Los Angeles: Archer.

— (2000) *The Age of Access: The New Culture of Hypercapitalism, Where All of Life Is a Paid-for Experience*, New York: Tarcher/Putnam.

— (1995) *The End of Work: The Decline of the Global Labor Force and the Dawn of the Post-Market Era, New York: G.P. Putnam's Sons.

Reich, Robert (1992) *The Work of Nations. Preparing Ourselves for 21st- Century Capitalism*, New York: Vintage.

Roodman, David (2012) *Due Diligence: An Impertinent Inquiry into Microfinance*, Washington: Center for Global Development.

Roose, Kevin (2014) 'The Sharing Economy Isn't About Trust, It's About Desperation', *New York Magazine*, 24 April, http://nymag.com/daily/intelligencer/2014/04/sharing-economy-is-about-desperation.html.

Rushkoff, Douglas (1994) *Cyberia. Life in the Trenches of Hyperspace*, New York: HarperCollins Publishers.

Safranski, Rüdiger (2009) *Romantik: Eine deutsche Affäre*, Frankfurt: Fischer.

Scheiber, Noam (2014) 'Silicon Valley Is Ruining "Sharing" for Everybody.

The Marketing Lie behind Companies Like Airbnb and Lyft', *New Republic*, 14 August, https://newrepublic.com/article/119072/silicon-valleys-sharing-economy-airbnb-lyft-are-selling-big-lie.

Schirrmacher, Frank (2014) 'Das Armband der Neelie Kroes', *Frankfurter Allgemeine Zeitung*, March 3rd,

http://www.faz.net/aktuell/feuilleton/debatten/ueberwachung/frank-schirrmacher-12826199.html?printPagedArticle=true#pageIndex_2.

Schmidt, Eric & Rosenberg, Jonathan (2014) *How Google Works*, London: John Murray.

Scholz, Trebor (2014) 'Platform Cooperativism vs. the Sharing Economy', *Medium*, 5 December, https://medium.com/@trebors/platform-cooperativism-vs-the-sharing-economy-2ea737f1b5ad#.giko449rt.

Schor, Juliet (2014) 'Debating the Sharing Economy', *Great Transition Initiative*, October, http://greattransition.org/publication/debating-the-sharing-economy.

Schulze, Gerhard (1992) *Erlebnisgesellschaft: Kultursoziologie der Gegenwart*, Frankfurt am Main: Campus.

Schumpeter, Joseph (1912) *Theorie der Wirtschaftlichen Entwicklung*, Leipzig: Duncker & Humblot.

Sennett, Richard (2008) *The Craftsman*, London: Allen Lane.

— (1977) *The Fall of Public Man*, New York: W.W. Norton & Co.

Serres, Michel (2012) *Petite Poucette*, Paris: Éditions Le Pommier.

— (2000) *The Birth of Physics*, trans. Jack Hawkes, Manchester: Clinamen Press.

Simmel, Georg (1999) 'Die Geselligkeit. Beispiel der Reinen oder Formalen Soziologie', in Otthein Rammstedt (ed.), *Gesamtausgabe, Vol. 16*, Frankfurt am Main: Suhrkamp, pp. 103-121.

Singer, Natasha (2014) 'In the Sharing Economy, Workers Find Both Freedom and Uncertainty', *The New York Times*, 16 August, http://www.nytimes.com/2014/08/17/technology/in-the-sharing-economy-workers-find-both-freedom-and-uncertainty.html?_r=0.

Slee, Tom (2015) *What's Yours Is Mine. Against the Sharing Economy*, New York: OR Books.

Sloterdijk, Peter (2009) *Du Mußt Dein Leben Ändern: Über Anthropotechnik*, Frankfurt am Main: Suhrkamp.

Smith, Heather (2014) 'The "Sharing" Economy Cozies Up to Subprime Auto Loans," *Grist.org*, Nov. 12: http://grist.org/business-technology/the-sharing-economy-cozies-up-to-subprime-auto-loans/.

Sorge, Arndt & van Witteloostuijn, Arjen (2004) 'The (Non)sense of Organizational Change: An Essay about Universal Management Hypes, Sick Consultancy Metaphors, and Healthy Organization Theories', Organization Studies, 25 (7), pp. 1205-1231.

Spinoza, Benedict de (1996) *Ethics*, ed. & trans. Edwin Curley, New York: Penguin Books.

Stiegler, Bernard (2015) *Symbolic Misery 2: The* katastrophē *of the Sensible*, trans. Barnaby Norman, Cambridge: Polity.

— (2014a) *Symbolic Misery 1: The Hyperindustrial Epoch*, trans. Barnaby Norman, Cambridge: Polity.

— (2014b) *Disbelief and Discredit 3: The Lost Spirit of Capitalism*, trans. Daniel Ross, Cambridge: Polity.

— (2014c) *States of Shock: Stupidity and Knowledge in the 21st Century*, trans. Daniel Ross, Cambridge: Polity.

— (2013) *What Makes Life Worth Living: On Pharmacology*, Cambridge: Polity.

— (2010a) *For a New Critique of Political Economy*, trans. Daniel Ross, Cambridge, Polity.

— (2010b) *Technics and Time, 3: Cinematic Time and the Question of Malaise*, trans. Stephen Barker, Stanford: Stanford University Press.

— (2010c) *Taking Care of Youth and the Generations*, trans. Daniel Ross, Stanford: Stanford University Press.

— (2009) *Technics and Time 2: Disorientation*, trans. Stephen Barker, Stanford: Stanford University Press.

— (1998) *Technics and Time 1: The Fault of Epimetheus*, trans. George Collins & Richard Beardsworth, Stanford: Stanford University Press.

Täubner, Mischa (2013) 'Zeigt her Eure Güte', *Brand Eins* (9), http://www.brandeins.de/archiv/2013/verhandeln/zeigt-her-eure-guete/.

Tarde, Gabriel (1993) *Les Lois de Imitation*, Texte de la Deuxième Edition 1895, Paris: Éditions Kimé.

— (1999) *Monadologie et Sociologie*, Paris: Institut Synthélabo.

Tanz, Jason (2014) 'How Airbnb and Lyft Finally Got Americans to Trust Each Other', *Wired*, 23 April, http://www.wired.com/2014/04/trust-in-the-share-economy/.

The Economist (2014) 'The Sharing Economy. Remove the Roadblocks', http://www.economist.com/news/leaders/21601257-too-many-obstacles-are-being-placed-path-people-renting-things-each-other-remove.

Thiel, Peter (2014) *Zero to One: Notes on Startups, or How to Build the Future*, London: Virgin Books.

Thrift, Nigel (2006) "Re-Inventing Invention: New Tendencies in Capitalist Commodification," *Economy and Society* 35(2), pp. 279-306.

Tiku, Nitasha (2014) 'Uber and Its Shady Partners Are Pushing Drivers into Subprime Loans', VALLEYWAG, Nov. 4: http://valleywag.gawker.com/uber-and-its-shady-partners-are-pushing-drivers-into-su-1649936785.

Tönnies, Ferdinand (1887) *Gemeinschaft und Gesellschaft. Abhandlung des Communismus und des Socialismus als empirischer Culturformen*. Leipzig: Fues Verlag.

Tsotsies, Alexa (2012) 'TaskRabbit Gets $13M From Founders Fund And Others To "Revolutionize The World's Labor Force"', *TechCrunch*, 23 July, http://techcrunch.com/2012/07/23/taskrabbit-gets-13m-from-founders-fund-and-others-to-revolutionize-the-worlds-labor-force/.

Ulam, Stanislaw (1958) 'Tribute to John von Neumann', *Bulletin of the American Mathematical Society*, 64 (3), pp. 1-49.

Van Abel, Bas; Klaassen, Roel; Evers, Lucas & Troxler, Peter (eds.) (2011) *Open Design Now. Why Design Cannot Remain Exclusive*, Amsterdam: BIS Publishers.

Van Andel, Pek & Bourcier, Danièle (2013) *De la Sérendipité dans la Science, la Technique, l'Art et le Droit: Leçons de l'Inattendu*, Paris: Editions Hermann.

— (1994) 'Anatomy of the Unsought Finding. Serendipity: Origin, History, Domains, Traditions, Appearances, Patterns and Programmability', *The British Journal for the Philosophy of Science*, 45 (2), pp. 631-648.

Venn, Couze; Boyne, Roy; Phillips, John & Bishop, Ryan (2007) 'Technics, Media, Teleology. Interview with Bernard Stiegler', *Theory, Culture & Society* 24 (7-8), pp. 334-341.

Vinge, Vernor (1993) 'The Coming Technological Singularity: How to Survive in the Post-Human Era', *Whole Earth Review (Winter)*, pp. 88-95.

Virilio, Paul (2007) *The Original Accident*, trans. Julie Rose, Cambridge: Polity.

— (1999) *The Politics of the Very Worst*, trans. Michael Cavaliere, ed. Silvère Lotringer, New York: Semiotext(e).

Virno, Paolo (2004) *A Grammar of the Multitude: For an Analysis of Contemporary Forms of Life*, trans. J. Cascaito I. Bertoletti, A. Casson, Los Angeles: Semiotext(e).

— (1996) 'Virtuosity and Revolution: The Political Theory of Exodus', in Paolo Virno and Michael Hardt (eds.), *Radical Thought in Italy: A Potential Politics*, Minneapolis: University of Minnesota Press, pp. 189-212.

Vonk, Oscarine (2014) "Creatieve Getto's" *Parool*, March 26: PS5.

Waber, Ben; Magnolfi, Jennifer & Lindsay, Greg (2014) 'Workspaces That Move People', *Harvard Business Review*, October, pp. 68-77.

Weber, Max (1976) *The Protestant Ethic and the Spirit of Capitalism*, London: Allen & Unwin.

Welzer, Harald (2013) *Selbst Denken: Eine Anleitung zum Widerstand*, Frankfurt am Main: Fischer.

— (2008) 'Überleben, aber wie?', *Die Zeit*, 17.04.' http://www.zeit.de/2008/17/Klimaanpassung.

Whyte, William Hollingsworth (1956) *The Organization Man*, New York: Simon & Schuster.

Wiener, Norbert (1961) *Cybernetics, or, Control and Communication in the Animal and the Machine*, 2nd ed., New York: MIT Press.

Wiener, Norbert; Bigelow, Julian and Rosenblueth, Arturo (1943) 'Behavior, Purpose and Teleology', *Philosophy of Science*, 10, pp. 18-24.

Wolfe, Tom (1968) *The Electric Kool-Aid Acid Test*, New York: Picador.

Wosskow, Debbie (2014) *Unlocking the sharing economy. An independent review*, Department for Business, Innovation and Skills. https://www.gov.uk/government/uploads/system/uploads/attachment_data/file/378291/bis-14-1227-unlocking-the-sharing-economy-an-independent-review.pdf.

Yglesias, Matthew (2013) 'There Is No "Sharing Economy"', *Slate Magazine*, Dec 13th, http://www.slate.com/blogs/moneybox/2013/12/26/myth_of_the_sharing_economy_there_s_no_such_thing.html.

Zola, Émile (2008) *The Ladies' Paradise*, trans. Brian Nelson, Oxford: Oxford World Classics.

Repeater Books

is dedicated to the creation of a new reality. The landscape of twenty-first-century arts and letters is faded and inert, riven by fashionable cynicism, egotistical self-reference and a nostalgia for the recent past. Repeater intends to add its voice to those movements that wish to enter history and assert control over its currents, gathering together scattered and isolated voices with those who have already called for an escape from Capitalist Realism. Our desire is to publish in every sphere and genre, combining vigorous dissent and a pragmatic willingness to succeed where messianic abstraction and quiescent co-option have stalled: abstention is not an option: we are alive and we don't agree.